God, The Meaning of Life, and What Happens After You Die

47 Extraordinary Stories From The After-Life: Near-Death Experiences, Past-Life Regressions, Psychic Channelling, And Secret Military Experiments On The Subconscious

God, The Meaning of Life, and What Happens After You Die

Copyright © 2017 Mark Anastasi. All rights reserved. No portion of this book, except for brief review, may be reproduced, stored in a retrieval system, or transmitted in any form or by any means—electronic, mechanical, photocopying, recording, or otherwise—without the written permission of the publisher.

Published by
Inspired Publishing Ltd
27 Old Gloucester Street
London
WC1N 3AX

Printed in the United Kingdom

ISBN: 978-1-78555-021-8

God, The Meaning of Life, and What Happens After You Die

DEDICATION

To my amazing wife Mira, for her unwavering support and love throughout the years. I am blessed to have you in my life. And to my daughters Mila and Zara, who inspired me to write this book.

God, The Meaning of Life, and What Happens After You Die

TABLE OF CONTENTS

Introduction 7

PART I: THE QUESTIONS 27

Chapter 1: Where Do We Come From? 29
Chapter 2: What Happens After We Die? 47
Chapter 3: What is The Meaning of Life? 71

PART II: THE STORIES 75

Chapter 4: When The Invisible World Meets The Visible World 77
Chapter 5: Past Lives 87
Chapter 6: The Miracle Man 97

PART III: THE INSIGHTS 121

Chapter 7: 10 Spiritual Insights That Will Change Your Life 123
Chapter 8: How To Win The Game of Life 159

FINAL THOUGHTS 161

APPENDIX 165

God, The Meaning of Life, and What Happens After You Die

Materialism, *noun*

1. A tendency to consider material possessions and physical comfort as more important than spiritual values.

2. The doctrine that nothing exists except matter and its movements and modifications.

INTRODUCTION

When I was 9 years old I read Raymond Moody's book, *Life After Life*. My mother had picked it up at her local book club, and I was intrigued by the title. Moody, an American psychologist, interviewed hundreds of people who had undergone near-death experiences, and presented his case studies.

The people he spoke to had been declared clinically dead, and following their resuscitation by paramedics or in a hospital reported very odd things indeed from their brief time in 'the spirit world'. For example, they remembered looking *down* at their body on the operating table, while floating above the scene; they felt drawn into 'the light' where they felt an overwhelming feeling of love and acceptance; and they were greeted in the spirit world by their 'spirit guide' and their loved ones who had passed away.

In many instances, while they were clinically dead, they became aware of things happening in a different part of the hospital, or even thousands of miles away. Their consciousness did not 'die' and was able to visit with—and read the thoughts of—their relatives halfway across the world. They later reported conversations they could not have possibly known.

Some of Moody's subjects stated, after 'visiting' the spirit world:

- *"Life is forever. Death is nothing more than a doorway. Something that you walk through... Death is a railroad station where you come, always, to go to another life. We cannot die because we are already created... to live forever."*

- *"In the spirit world you feel an overwhelming feeling of love and acceptance. I would exchange twenty lifetimes for a few moments in the presence of that love* and acceptance... <u>You are so deeply loved and you yourself so deeply love</u>. Love is what keeps this world alive. We are alive because of love."

- "When you return to the spirit world from whence you came, you begin to sense a part of yourself greater and far more magnificent than you ever give yourself credit for. <u>You are a part of All That Is, and so is everyone else</u>. As a result, you become a lot more understanding of others."

- "Upon returning to the spirit world you are asked: How did you learn to love and accept your fellow humans in the way Source totally accepts and loves you?"

I had so many questions! If we go to a spiritual realm after we die, do we *come* from one as well? Are we spiritual beings having a human experience? What does this mean about how we should live our lives? Why are we *here*? What is 'Source'? What is '*All That Is*'?

"There really *is* life after death!" I concluded, upon reading Moody's book. Our consciousness goes on beyond the point of death. What baffled me what this: "*How on Earth do grown-ups not talk about this all the time?!*" Every day, they get up, go to work, come home, watch TV, and go to sleep. At no point do they seem to question their existence or their origin. Perhaps they are too busy with their jobs to notice that their lives lack meaning.

I couldn't understand why these questions weren't being asked every single day in the news or on every TV program. In fact, the media seemed to do their utmost to steer people *away* from such questions. I would later discover that it was considered 'blasphemous' to raise this topic because reincarnation was not mentioned in the Bible, the Torah, or the Koran, despite millions of people around the world having profound, personal spiritual experiences that contradicted these religious teachings.

My parents were atheists. To them, religion was for ignorant, 'uneducated' people, and the cause of most wars, to boot. So I let it go. I forgot about Moody's book. I didn't believe in God. Over the ensuing decade I focused on getting good grades, getting a job, and getting ahead in life.

Introduction

Physical Matter Is Not... *Real*

My interest in spirituality was reignited in my twenties after stumbling upon books on Quantum Physics. Scientists in the 1920s had discovered that all the physical matter in our Universe... *is not real.* The atoms that make up physical matter consist of empty space with a pattern of energy running through it. There's nothing *solid* within the atoms that make up physical reality! There was a 'meta-physical' aspect to our physical reality after all, they concluded, and even went as far as comparing our universe to a giant 'thought' (one singular unifying consciousness). In fact, they found that *consciousness* was central to the workings of physical reality and that our thoughts can affect the physical matter around us.

This new science flew in the face of conventional Newtonian physics and its materialistic viewpoint ('materialism' is the doctrine that nothing exists except matter and its movements and modifications), and made many scientists question their assumptions about our universe. The ideological divide between science and religion was beginning to blur. This was a threat to the legitimacy of 'modern science'. A *'war on consciousness'* would have to be waged, to maintain their status and power. The less people focused on spirituality, the more power the Scientific Elite would garner.

In the book *The Celestine Prophecy*, author James Redfield describes the new spiritual awareness that was beginning to take hold, away from traditional religious or scientific dogmas. He wrote in 1993:

> *"We're re-discovering a whole new depth to what our existence means. We are beginning to sense that there is another side to life – an 'invisible' side to life, a process operating behind the scenes. In the twentieth century, we began to realize that faster, better, more... was* not *the answer. People with all the fame, success, and money in the world STILL did not feel a sense of inner peace and fulfilment.* <u>Time has come to wake up from our illusion and our concern for economic security and scientific progress, and re-consider that original question: Why are we really here?</u>
>
> *[...] In 1,000 AD, the powerful churchmen held great influence over the minds of people. Everything about life was, above all, spiritual. People's reality was that God's plan for mankind was at the very center of life. People took for granted that the world operated solely by spiritual means. Then, around the 14th and 15th century, that reality began to break down.*

Corruption, theft, greed, and all kinds of improprieties by these churchmen led to alarm in the minds of people and then to outright rebellion. These men, who had been the only connection between yourself and God, and the arbitrators of your salvation, had suddenly lost all credibility.

The consensus about the nature of the universe and mankind's purpose here was collapsing. The old world view was being challenged even further when astronomers in the 1600s proved that the sun and the stars did not revolve around the Earth, as maintained by the Church. The whole world was being thrown into question. People no longer blindly accepted the scriptures – they wanted solid proof and answers. They therefore turned to Science.

People lost their sense of certainty about who they are and where they came from approximately four centuries ago. <u>Ever since they have strived for progress, conquering the planet, raising their standard of living and sense of security… to replace the spiritual security they had lost.</u> This has not brought us the happiness and peace of mind we so long for. <u>Is it any surprise? We have been ignoring our very essence</u>.

Our aim was to create an understanding of the universe that made the world seem safe and manageable. Science systematically removed the esoteric from our model of the world. The preoccupation of why we are here, and who we really are, spiritually, was cast aside and repressed. <u>We forgot that we still don't know what we're surviving for. Why are we here? Where are we going?</u>"

To this day 'Science' has not been able to provide answers to these fundamental questions, so central to our existence.

The Four Great Philosophical Questions

"Who are we? Where do we come from? What should we do? Where are we going? These are the four great questions that everybody faces, whether they realize it or not. And if you don't answer these four great questions, obviously your life is pretty meaningless. And many people just stuff those questions down. They want the answers made for them. They want somebody like Jesus, or Krishna, or Buddha, or someone else to do it for them. It can't be done. It's like wanting someone else to be born for you, or to die for you, or to eat your lunch for you. These things are inescapably personal."

Miceal Ledwith, PhD, Professor of Systematic Theology, Maynooth College

"A Few Year Ago I Died Crossing This Street!"

Over the years, I came across people whose personal experiences seemed to confirm that there is, indeed, life after death. During one of my talks in London in 2011, a woman came up to me at the break. Her name was Veronique. She was a French architect, in her fifties, who had travelled from France to attend. The seminar was taking place just off High Street Kensington, and she said, *"You know, this is quite a coincidence, because a few years ago I DIED crossing this very street…"*.

In 1997, Veronique was living in London. She was crossing that very road we were on, in front of the Whole Foods Market building, when a large, speeding motorcycle ran her down. She remembers floating above the scene, seeing the paramedics put a white sheet over her body, and pronouncing her dead! She explains:

> *"I felt myself float upwards. I could still make out the contours of my hands. As I floated higher than the five-story Victorian building, I remember thinking to myself 'the architecture of this building is very interesting…'. As I kept floating higher, I could no longer make out my body. I was just light. Soon, I was surrounded by beings of light. They told me that my time had not come yet, and that they would store information in my mind and give me certain abilities that would be unlocked at the appropriate time. I was then sent back down what I can only describe as a tube of light, and I awoke back in my body, in the ambulance. The paramedics could not believe it. They called it a miracle."*

Veronique has since developed interesting healing abilities, which she describes as being 'akin to those of a shaman'.

My neighbour Louis, a Cypriot man, told me of his near-death experience over a glass of homemade lemonade one summer, in Cyprus. When he was seven years old, in the 1950s, he and his family left the island and emigrated to England. Soon thereafter he contracted a disease and was rushed to hospital. At one point his heart stopped, and the nurses and doctors on staff tried desperately to revive him.

"I was floating above the whole scene, in the corner of the ceiling. I then kept floating upwards, <u>through</u> the ceiling! I remember hearing one of the beings say, in an annoyed manner, 'No, no, no. It's not his time yet! Send him back!' The next thing I knew I was back in my body. Since that experience, I am no longer afraid of dying."

During a past-life regression, under hypnosis, my American friend Stewart recalled being in the spirit world, prior to being reincarnated:

"I felt myself glide upward in a funnel of light where I was soon met by beautiful angelic beings who gently took my hands. The rest is all a blur. There was a review of my life, a glimpse of my past lives, a period of mourning for all the wrong that I had done, and a happy feeling for all of the good that I had accomplished. Then I was told I had to complete something on Earth. I was shown a woman in labour in a brand new hospital. The next thing I knew, I was inside a tube of light heading toward her."

These first-hand experiences confirmed to me the existence of a spirit world. Most people I meet nowadays have had or know of someone who has had an out-of-body experience, a near-death experience, or some other spiritual or metaphysical experience. But most people tend to dismiss such events, because they don't fit in with the prevalent Philosophy of Materialism (and Philosophy of Futility) promoted by mainstream media.

> *"The reason vast numbers of people can't answer questions like 'who are we', 'where are we going', and 'what are we doing here' is because the control system is structured so that from cradle to grave that knowledge is suppressed and kept from them."*
>
> David Icke

Cultivating a Philosophy of Futility Is Good For The Ruling Class

By the 1950s, every corporation and advertising agency in America had psychoanalysts on their payroll. They called them 'the depth boys'. Their role was to develop techniques to get inside and manage the unconscious mind of the consumer. One of their discoveries was that <u>to increase sales to the public, the consumer must be permanently dissatisfied</u>.

Erich Fromm was a German social psychologist and philosopher. According to Fromm, the consumer must be permanently dissatisfied, or gratified only for the shortest possible time. <u>Satisfaction would stop consumption, which would stall economic growth</u>. Consider how in today's society we are conditioned through advertising to constantly want and desire the latest automobile model. The latest fashion. The latest gadget. And we are made to feel like 'losers' if we don't own it.

Planned obsolescence is another strategy used by corporations to keep consumers buying more and more. Planned obsolescence in industrial design is a policy of planning or designing a product with an artificially limited useful life, so it will become obsolete, unfashionable, or no longer functional after a certain period of time.

We have been conditioned to throw out the old and buy the new, in the name of fashion and appearing 'cool' to others. We must keep up with the Joneses, or else we're looked down on by society. This is a mental construct created by advertising. But it *becomes* real in our society, because people are suckered in by the programming.

> "Nearly half of what people in the West hear, see, or read is written by professional liars. Professional liars whose job it is to keep people in front of their televisions, reading gossip magazines, eating vast amounts of toxic food, and shopping... always shopping for the latest fashions and trends. [...] Anything that keeps the masses from organizing themselves and asking important questions about what their masters are really up to."
>
> *Propaganda* (2012 documentary)

It wasn't enough though for consumers to merely be *dissatisfied*. Psychologists discovered that <u>if people believe their lives to be empty and meaningless they are much more likely to fill that void through mindless consumption</u>. Buying something would satisfy them for a short while. In a world without spiritual beliefs, such nihilism is ripe.

> Nihilism: the rejection of all religious and moral principles, in the belief that life is meaningless.

'Philosophy of futility' is a phrase coined by Columbia University marketing professor Paul Nystrom in 1938 to describe the disposition caused by the monotony of the new industrial age. Nystrom observed that the natural effect of this malaise (the 'Philosophy of Futility') was <u>seeking gratification found in frivolous things</u>, such as fashionable goods.

He claimed that this tendency in the modern world could be manipulated to induce a vicious circle of dissatisfaction and the desire for new consumer goods, thereby increasing sales. <u>This lack of purpose in life has a powerful effect on consumption: people buy stuff in order to feel happier.</u> If your life feels 'empty', you shop 'til you drop.

Nystrom wrote in his book *Economics of Fashion*:

> *"Most people in western nations have departed from old-time standards of religion and philosophy, and having failed to develop forceful views to take their places, hold to something that may be called 'a philosophy of futility'. This view of life (or lack of a view of life) involves a question as to the value of motives and purposes of the main human activities. There is ever a tendency to challenge the purpose of life itself. This lack of purpose in life has an effect on consumption similar to that of having a narrow life interest, that is, in concentrating human attention on the more superficial things that comprise much of fashionable consumption."*

When people don't hold onto any spiritual beliefs, they'll believe anything. They adopt a 'Philosophy of Futility': my life doesn't matter, nothing I do really matters, <u>I feel empty inside, my life feels empty… so I might as well buy more stuff</u>…

> *"We must shift America from a 'needs' to a 'desires' culture. People must be trained to desire, to want new things even before the old had been entirely consumed. We must shape a new mentality in America. Man's desires must overshadow his needs."*
>
> Wall Street banker Paul Mazer of Lehman Brothers, 1930

What better way to develop a sense of futility in people than to deny the existence of life after death, God, or anything spiritual? Television and the media conglomerates—owned and controlled by the largest corporations and banks in the world—seem hell-bent on removing spiritual matters from our consciousness, while promoting at every turn atheists such as Richard Dawkins, Christopher Hitchens, Professor Brian Cox, Bill Nye 'The Science Guy', etc.

The Philosophy of Futility is cultivated and programmed into our society in a thousand subtle ways, through television shows, movies, magazines.

> "From infancy we have drilled into us that we need to adopt a philosophy of futility and that we have to perceive ourselves as passive consumers. [...] The goal for the corporations is to maximise profit and market share. [The population] have to be turned into completely mindless consumers of goods that they do not want. You have to develop what are called "Creative Wants". You have to impose on people what's called a Philosophy of Futility. You have to focus them on the insignificant things of life, like fashionable consumption. I'm just basically quoting business literature. The ideal is to have individuals who are totally disassociated from one another, whose conception of themselves, their sense of value is just "how many created wants can I satisfy?" The public relations industry and advertising are designed to mould people into this desired pattern from infancy."
>
> Noam Chomsky, *Manufacturing Consent*

Every avenue is used to pursue this agenda. TED talks now routinely censor scientists who share ideas on consciousness. Rupert Sheldrake's talk titled *The Science Delusion* was banned, after he exposed the delusion of modern-day science—the delusion that our bodies, our minds and indeed our entire universe are nothing but physical stuff. *'Materialism'* is the fairytale on which nearly all of modern science is based, and yet materialism is a delusion. He stated: *"The science delusion is the belief that science already understands the nature of reality, leaving only the details to be filled in."*

Cultivating a 'Philosophy of Futility' within our society and removing spiritual values from it has been and remains to this day a primary objective of the ruling class. The result: people feel depressed, isolated, and 'empty inside'. Why? Because they are ignoring *'their very essence'*.

> *"I sometimes feel like I'm just doomed to walk around in and out of TGI Friday's with this emptiness I can't quite put my finger on."*
>
> Bill Burr, comedian

How can we even begin to know how to live, or what is important in life, if we don't know where we come from or what happens *after* we've lived? How can we truly experience *meaning* in our lives?

Advertising Exploits Your Emotional Vulnerabilities And Steers You Away From What Really Makes You Happy

Advertising unashamedly fosters unhappiness with oneself and with one's possessions. In fact, the very purpose of advertising is to make people feel that without this or that product you are inferior ('less than', not good enough, not cool) and defective (what's wrong with you?!).

In the words of a contemporary advertising executive, "Advertising at its best is about making people feel that without their product, you're a loser... You open up emotional vulnerabilities."

If you are constantly made to feel 'Not Good Enough', you buy more stuff. This is particularly glaring in women's magazines. In Jean Kilbourne's excellent book *Can't Buy My Love*, she makes the following observations about advertising:

- ❑ Advertising is one of the most powerful forces in our society. Advertising is part of the environment you live in, and this environment has been *polluted*.
- ❑ Advertising shapes our values, our attitudes, our culture, and defines our dreams, *even if we don't think it works on us*. We are all influenced by advertising. There is no way to tune out this much

- ❏ information, especially when it is designed to break through the 'tuning out' process.
- ❏ The bankrupt values of advertising —organized around money and driven by hype— corrupt our true values, relationships, and commitment to civic life.
- ❏ Ads create an environment in which bad choices are constantly reinforced (addiction, fast food, smoking and drinking, narcissism and selfishness, etc.).
- ❏ Ads reinforce that human relationships are fragile, difficult, and disappointing but products won't let us down. *("Who says guys are afraid of commitment? He's had the same backpack for years."; "The ski instructor faded away three years ago, but the sweater didn't.";* to children: *"This toy doll is your new best friend!")*
- ❏ <u>The main message of advertising is that happiness comes from products, *not* relationships.</u>
- ❏ Advertising corrupts relationships and then offers us products as solace and as substitutes for human connection we long for.
- ❏ Ads encourage us to objectify each other and to believe that our most significant relationships are with products. Ads leave us romantic about objects and deeply cynical about humans.
- ❏ Advertising contributes greatly to a climate in which relationships flounder and addictions flourish. Relationships are constantly devalued. Kilbourne writes: "<u>I believe there is a connection between the throwaway world of advertising and today's throwaway approach to marriage</u>. All too often our market-driven culture locks people into adolescent fantasies of sex and relationships. And there is a connection between the constant images of instant sexual gratification and passion and the increasing burden on marriage and long-term lovers."
- ❏ Advertisers use psychological research to target children (because if you hook them early, they are yours for life).
- ❏ "I am raising my daughter in a culture that is entirely materialistic, that co-opts spiritual values and movements for social change and uses them to sell her jeans and cigarettes. I am raising her in a culture that trivializes relationships and encourages her to envy her friends and compete with them."

- "Our materialistic culture encourages [suffering from a sense of emptiness] because people who feel empty make great consumers. The emptier we feel, the more likely we are to turn to products, to fill us up, to make us feel whole … They all serve to distance us from our feelings and to deflect attention from that which might really make a difference in our lives."
- Ads steer us away from what really makes us happy: "meaningful work, authentic relationships, and a sense of connection with history, community, nature, and the cosmos."

> **Creating A Model That Is Virtually Impossible To Attain**
>
> *"Infotainment is used for programming and conditioning the public. This medium is far more effective for subliminal reinforcement of desired attitudes towards our objectives. We reinforce the desired norm through advertising, creating a model for people to live up to, that is virtually impossible to attain. The result is an incomplete, desperate individual seeking acceptance."*
>
> American media insider

Depression Is a Rational Response To a Sick Society

I believe that the values of materialism promoted by mass media today (to the detriment of spiritual values), and the resultant loss of belief in God or the afterlife, are to blame for the surge in instances of depression. The Advertising industry and mass media have subverted and corrupted our traditional values. They have perverted and corrupted every aspect of our daily life, for the sake of promoting 'consumerism'.

British psychologist Oliver James's research points to the fact that the era of 'Selfish Capitalism' unleashed by mass media advertising in the 1930s caused an epidemic of the 'Affluenza' virus. This is what he calls the set of values we see today in Western people, such as placing a high value on acquiring money and possessions, looking good in the eyes of others, and wanting to be famous (essentially, materialistic values which lead to egregious consumption). It is useful to remember that these values are not innate to human beings. They've *been programmed into us*. Oliver writes:

> *"Infection with the Affluenza Virus increases your susceptibility to the commonest emotional distresses: depression, anxiety, substance abuse and personality disorders (e.g. 'me, me, me' narcissism, febrile moods, or confused identity). [...] We have become absolutely obsessed with measuring ourselves and others through the distorted lens of Affluenza values. The great majority of people in English-speaking nations now define their lives through earnings, possessions, appearance and celebrity, and those things are making them miserable because they impede the meeting of our fundamental needs."*

In other words, <u>the more materialistic a society becomes, the more its inhabitants become depressed, anxious, and they don't know who they even are anymore</u>.

A 2004 study by the World Health Organization highlighted the shocking fact that over 26% of Americans had suffered from some form of emotional distress in the previous 12 months (such as depression, anxiety, substance abuse), SIX times more than Nigerians, who were forty times poorer than America. America, he notes, is by some margin the most emotionally distressed of all nations.

Oliver James presents two interesting conclusions. The first is that depression and anxiety are normal in a society bombarded by unfettered advertising and consumeristic values:

> *"It is grossly inaccurate to depict depression, anxiety, and other psychoses as diseases requiring medical treatment. [...] <u>most emotional distress is best understood as a rational response to sick societies</u>. Change those societies, and we will all be less distressed."*

In other words, change the *environment*, and depression and anxiety will become rarer occurrences. There are 350 million people suffering from depression around the world, according to the World Health Organization, and this is not caused by some 'chemical imbalance' in their brains. **This is caused by the fact that our society is profoundly sick and corrupted.**

His second conclusion is even more poignant: religion or spiritual beliefs can immunize people against the effects of this materialistic 'virus'. Indeed, <u>people who believe in something beyond our physical world are far less likely to suffer from depression and unhappiness</u>.

> *"Wherever I went I found that religion seemed to be a powerful vaccine. Much to the consternation of social scientists, on average, regular churchgoers suffer less depression or unhappiness than unbelievers. Almost by definition, religious people are less likely to be materialistic and to have Virus goals or motivations and more likely to be preoccupied with things spiritual. One study of 860 young American adults, showed this very clearly. <u>Those with materialistic values, such as wanting money or prestige, were far less likely to be religious, and they were unhappier</u>, drank and smoked more, and, in the case of the women, were at greater risk of eating disorders."*

No surprise there, since people afflicted by a 'Philosophy of Futility' and materialistic values tend to use consumption to fill the spiritual void they are feeling. But you cannot consume your way to happiness.

> *"Most Americans today simply do not have anything to live for. They chase one form of entertainment after another, hoping that something will eventually fill the gaping holes that are constantly aching inside their hearts."*
>
> Michael Snyder, *The End Of The American Dream Blog*

> *"The widespread depression and anxiety created by the Affluenza Virus are crucial for Selfish Capitalism. To fill the emptiness and loneliness, and to replace our need for authentic, intimate relationships, we resort to consumption. The more anxious or depressed we are, the more we must consume, and the more we consume, the more disturbed we become."*
>
> Oliver James, psychologist, author of *"Affluenza"*

Spirituality Helps Societies Move Forward And Survive

Yuri Bezmenov is a former KGB officer who defected to the West in 1970. He revealed in a series of lectures in the 1980s the methods of ideological subversion (*"psychological warfare"*) used by the KGB to undermine the USA and other targeted countries. He explained that subversion involves undermining the religion, political system, and economic system of a country, for the purpose of destroying your enemy from within. To achieve their aims of transforming a nation from a democracy to a totalitarian 'communist regime' you needed to first *destroy the moral fabric of that nation*. Removing spirituality from the lives of people is a fundamental pillar of this psychological warfare, he explained.

Bezmenov claimed that 85% of activities carried out by the KGB were subversion tactics. 'Spying', while romanticized by James Bond movies, was only a small part of what the KGB was about.

The first stage of "Ideological Subversion" involves *demoralizing* a society. This can take up to 20 years to achieve. Once this process is complete, the next stage is 'destabilization'. This takes two to five years. The third stage involves bringing about a "crisis", and then finally 'normalizing' the situation through an armed invasion, for example. The name of the game was to defeat the U.S. through psychological manipulation; as Nikita Khrushchev warned the U.S.: *"We will bury you without firing a shot!"*.

The KGB's psychologists found that promoting *atheism* was the most effective tool for destroying traditionally-held values and therefore weaken a country from within (together with 'feminism', and 'liberalism'). Bezmenov outlined the following techniques for 'demoralizing a nation' and breaking down a society:

- ❑ Promote **Atheism**: convince people they are no different than any other animal and that they have no special, or divine right to existence. They are just 'accidents'. This is part of the demoralization process. Eliminate prayer or any type of religious expression in the schools on the grounds that it violates the principle of separation of church and state. With no real basis of morality, there is no real basis from which to seek the truth and argue for it.

- ❏ Promote **feminism** to create discontent in women and hasten the breakup of families, the "blood cells" of a society.

- ❏ Break down **cultural standards of morality** by promoting pornography, obscenity, and violence in books, magazines, movies, radio, and TV. Promote homosexuality, 'gay rights', and 'alternative lifestyles' under the guise of 'liberalism' and 'progressivism', to promote a culture of 'anything goes' and hasten moral decay.

- ❏ Promote **sexual promiscuity** in women: with no morals to uphold, and nothing sacred, men have nothing to fight for. "Nothing destroys a nation faster."

- ❏ Increase **self-indulgence** and reduce self-reliance: push people in the direction they are already going... give them more and more of what they want... junk food, pornography, entertainment, free welfare money... to increase self-indulgence.

- ❏ If you want teenagers to have sex, have 'Sex Ed' classes at school. If you want teenagers to start doing drugs, have 'Drug Ed' classes at school. If you want teenagers to start drinking, have 'Alcohol Ed' at school.

- ❏ Promote **immigration** and multi-culturalism: This destroys feelings of patriotism. Native people will not feel *'as if it's their country anymore'*, so they won't feel like fighting to protect it; this is why you won't ever hear of multiculturalism being foisted on China or Israel.

I will let you, the reader, make up your own mind as to whether this process of cultural subversion has been carried out and its effects felt throughout Western civilization...

Bezmenov went on to say that this slow, gradual process of demoralization was intended to "change the perception of reality of every American to such an extent that despite the abundance of information, no one is able to come to sensible conclusions in the interests of defending themselves, their families, their community and their country. It is a brainwashing process which goes very slow." Fifteen years is the minimum time required to educate one generation of students in the country of your enemy.

Bezmenov explained in his lectures that many of the intellectuals teaching in American universities were trained in 'socialist' thinking. "Most of the people who graduated in the '60s are now occupying the positions of power. You are stuck with them. You cannot get rid of them. They are contaminated. They are programmed to think and react to certain stimuli in a certain pattern. You cannot change their mind even if you expose them to authentic information, even if you prove it, you still cannot change the basic perception and the logical behaviour. [...] The demoralization process in the United States is basically completed already. Demoralization now reaches such areas where previously, not even Comrade Andropov and all his experts would even dream of such a tremendous success. Thanks to a lack of moral standards. Exposure to true information does not matter anymore. A person who is demoralized is unable to assess true information. The facts tell nothing to him."

Bezmenov concluded his lectures by stating that the subversion and demoralization of a nation is easy to reverse, by restricting the import of propaganda, and **by bringing back society to spiritual values:**

> *"The History of socialist countries (countries with centralized power and pyramidal structure of power, civilizations like Egypt, the Mayans, Incas, Babylonian culture) ... they collapsed and disappeared from the surface of Earth the moment they lost religion. It's as simple as that. They disintegrated. All the sophisticated technology and computers will not prevent societies from disintegrating and eventually dying out. <u>Something that is NOT MATERIAL moves society and helps it to survive</u>. The moment we turn to something like '2×2=4' (materialistic principles) and make it a guiding principle of our existence... we die. Even though this is true... and this over here we cannot prove, we can only feel... and have faith..."*

> *"I don't believe in God, but I'm not an atheist, I just don't care. I don't have any real quest for God in my heart – though I'm a very good consumer – <u>because I can't deny the hole exists</u>.*
>
> *[...] I don't have a God in place and it just doesn't seem to concern me... I'll just deal with my weird discomfort existentially with masturbating, food, and movies. Just keep feeding the hole... Isn't that what being American is all about?"*
>
> Marc Maron, an American comedian who has spoken openly of living with severe depression most of his life.

Why I Wrote This Book

<u>Despite our purchasing power and incomes having risen five-fold since the 1950s, we are not any happier</u> (source: Professor Richard Layard of the London School of Economics). This is an astonishing fact. It should make us reconsider not only how we live our life but also how our society is structured. Governments' focus on 'GDP growth at all costs' is suicidal. It is not leading to widespread health, happiness and contentment. It is leading to concentration of wealth in the hands of a few and widespread poverty and inequality.

Perhaps the fact that 350 million people worldwide suffer from depression is not a surprise, considering how we have been ignoring our very essence—*we are spiritual beings having a physical experience*. Ignoring the spiritual truth of who we are inevitably leads to a state of depression, anxiety, and 'feeling lost'.

We used to value friendship, honour, valour, and courage. We used to value community, comradeship. Now, advertising has taught us to value fame, good looks, money, and status instead. We are taught to compete with one another in a 'dog-eat-dog' world, and to try to *'keep up with the Joneses'*. We are 'divided and conquered'. As a result, we mistrust one another. We don't even know our neighbours anymore, while sitting at our computer obsessing about our social media 'friends' and 'likes'.

Everything in our modern society has become superficial and fake. There isn't much substance to anything anymore. The trivial and mundane is celebrated. 'Celebrities' are elevated to cult-like status. We are being entertained and distracted to death. We are saturated with 'information', and yet receive no real wisdom. The media focus our attention on concerns such as 'looking good' and 'being popular'. This toxic 'mind-space' instils values that lead inexorably to a vacuous and meaningless existence.

> "Just look at us. Everything is backwards; everything is upside down. Doctors destroy health, lawyers destroy justice, universities destroy knowledge, psychiatrists destroy minds, scientists destroy truth, major media destroys information, religions destroy spirituality, and governments destroy freedom."
>
> Michael Ellner, author of *Hope Is Realistic*

The materialistic programming we are bombarded with (*sex, money, food, consumption, instant gratification*) has created the perfect 'consumer society' that benefits large corporations, but it corrupts our way of life. It guides us away from our innate human values and from our purpose. By chasing materialistic values we are no longer true to *our own* values. Depression, anxiety, and other mental disorders are the price we pay.

Why write this book now? Because people need a different life philosophy than the *'Philosophy of Futility'* and *'Doctrine of Materialism'* brainwashed into them from childhood. When I ask my childhood friends "Where do you think we come from?", or "Do you know what happens after we die?" I often get a shrug of the shoulders followed by "*Bah…I don't know…*"

I wrote this book as an antidote for people who feel 'lost' and depressed. One of the best compliments I ever received was from a student at a 'Liberty & Entrepreneurship' Camp in 2014, who said to me: *"Mark, how do you do it? You always seem so calm, peaceful, and smiling!"* Knowing the truth about our spiritual origins, life after death and the meaning of life makes one practically immune to those feelings of sadness and 'feeling lost'. They are replaced instantly by feelings of love, contentment, inner peace, and gratitude for this incredible gift that is life.

A New Spiritual Awareness

Who are we? Where do we come from? Why are we here? And where are we going?

To find answers to these fundamental questions, I decided to sidestep religious texts entirely—for reasons that will become apparent in this book—and instead I sought out people's *personal, 'direct' spiritual experiences* instead.

Near-death experiences, past-life regressions, secret military experiments on the subconscious of soldiers, experiences with consciousness-altering plants such as Ayahuasca and DMT, and information channelled directly from the spirit world, were just a few of my unorthodox sources.

Could these 'alternative' sources of spiritual information enlighten us as to where we come from and why we are here? Can this knowledge help people overcome the 'emptiness' they feel in their lives?

In *Part I* of this book I reveal some compelling answers to the 'Great Philosophical Questions' of where we come from, why we are here, and what happens after we die.

In *Part II*, I share personal stories and spiritual experiences from my own life—moments when the 'invisible' world made itself known in my physical reality.

Part III is titled *10 Spiritual Insights That Will Change Your Life*. It highlights the wisdom and lessons drawn from the information contained in this book, with practical advice on how to experience a renewed sense of joy and peace in our lives.

May this book bring you the answers, solace, and peace of mind you've been looking for.

PART I

The Questions

CHAPTER 1

Where Do We Come From?

The first and most important philosophical question we can ask ourselves is *'Where do we come from?'*

In our secular, modern world, so steeped in materialism, talk of the existence of God raises smirks, ridicule, and even contempt. While many people have rejected religion due to the corruption and misdeeds of the religious institutions over the centuries (to say nothing of their often contradictory texts), **this has led many to reject spirituality as well.** They have thrown the baby out with the bathwater, so to speak. But religions and spirituality are two distinct things. Just because I do not follow any specific religious 'dogma' or institution does not mean that I do not believe in the existence of God.

Perhaps the real problem lies in our understanding of what God *is*. Although the majority of Westerners are atheists, their idea of 'God' is that of *"a white man with a beard sitting on a cloud"* – an idea that comes from the very religions and religious imagery they have contempt for.

But what if 'God' is nothing like that? What if God is much, much *more* than that? What if God is an *intelligence,* a *consciousness* that transcends physical matter?

A Brief Lesson In Physics

Atoms are the basic building blocks of physical matter. Atoms are very small: a grain of sand consists of 100 *quintillion* (100,000,000,000,000,000,000) atoms, to give you an idea of how *tiny* atoms are.

Hydrogen and Helium atoms make up 98% of all the matter in the universe. Your desk, bed, house, computer, houseplants—in fact *everything* you see around you—are made of atoms. Even the air you breathe is made of atoms (N_2, CO_2 and O_2). *You* are made up of atoms (Carbon and Hydrogen, primarily).

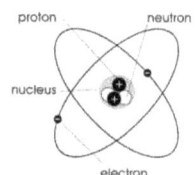

Atoms consist of a nucleus, which contains neutrons and protons (positively charged), and the electrons spinning around it (negatively charged). These electrons spin around the nucleus at huge distances from it – comparatively to the tiny size of the nucleus. The atom therefore consists of mostly empty space, surrounded by an electromagnetic force caused by the spinning electrons.

In reality, electrons don't *really* move around the nucleus... what they *actually* do is pop in and out of existence around the nucleus. They exist in one spot, then they don't, then they reappear in another spot, and then disappear again out of physical reality. *Where do they go when they are not part of our physical reality?*

Scientists were convinced that if they looked close enough, they would eventually find something *solid* within atoms, which would explain our 'solid matter' physical universe. As scientists looked closer and closer at the structure of the atom, they could only observe a physical void. *Empty space!* They *still* couldn't find anything solid! They came to the realization that <u>atoms have no physical structure</u>. They are merely vortices of energy, vibrating at different frequencies. This extraordinary mystery has prompted Quantum Physicists to state that *there is nothing physical or solid to what we perceive to be physical matter.* <u>The physical objects you observe around you are not *real*</u>. Only your *senses* (your consciousness!) make you *perceive it* as being 'real'!

Quantum Physicists postulated that physical matter *appears* solid because these particles are spinning so fast that it gives us the illusion that matter is real.

Although our senses make us think that something is solid (we *perceive* matter to be real), the particles that make up our physical reality are *not* solid or 'physical'. Your reality is formed by how electrical signals are being interpreted by your brain. Your body takes in this vibrational information encoded in photons of light, turns it into electrical signals, passes it on to your brain, and your brain then decodes that information as a world that appears to be solid. The illusion of 'solid matter' is quite astonishing, when seen in this light.

Do we live in 'The Matrix'?

As bizarre as all this may sound, the next discovery they made was *even weirder*. Scientists declared that these atoms are not *separate* patterns of energy, but instead are part of *a unified field of energy*. All particles in the universe are part of *one* energy, and they are all therefore connected to each other. Some physicists have stated they can only compare this unified field of energy to *'a thought-wave'*. Well, whose thought-wave could it be? *Could this be the Supreme Intelligence, or 'God-Mind' that mystics have spoken of since the dawn of time?*

Unable to marry their belief system with these groundbreaking discoveries, many scientists chose to cling to the old, materialistic, 'Newtonian' scientific worldview, and reject Quantum Physics. They could not accept the possibility of *Consciousness* or *Intelligence* (something metaphysical) being integral to the workings of physical reality and therefore physics. It would give their ideological enemy (religion) too much ammunition, and would undermine their very 'raison d´être'. After all, our society gave power, status and *funding* to scientific institutions from the 1600s onwards *because* they no longer trusted in religions' metaphysical explanation for our physical reality!

> *"Everything we call real is made of things that cannot be regarded as real. If quantum mechanics hasn't profoundly shocked you, you haven't understood it yet."*
>
> Niels Bohr, Danish Physicist

Spooky Action at A Distance

The experiments conducted by quantum physicists gave rise to *an even more baffling result*: any time they attempted to measure the property of a particle—e.g. position, momentum, spin, polarization, etc.—their thoughts were found to *act* on that particle. In other words, scientists' intentions and thoughts were altering the physical properties of the atoms they were observing! As James Redfield explains:

> *"Another major shift occurred in the mid-twentieth century, through the findings of quantum mechanics and Albert Einstein. Science could now prove that what we perceive as hard matter is mostly empty space with a pattern of energy running through it. Furthermore, experiments show that the act of observation of the elementary particles of this energy actually alters the results! This means that the basic 'stuff' of the Universe is <u>a pure energy that is malleable to human intention and expectation</u>!"*

This discovery implied that the scientists and the particles they were observing were somehow *connected,* and furthermore, those particles were exhibiting *intelligence* or 'consciousness'. Astoundingly, this transfer of information was occurring instantaneously, with no lapse of time, even if the particles being observed and the scientists performing the experiments were *thousands of miles* apart from each other. Albert Einstein would call this *"spooky action at a distance"*, and it flew in the face of conventional scientific thinking. And yet it would later be verified through further scientific experiments. The spiritual implications were earth-shattering. According to Wikipedia:

> "It appears that one particle of an entangled pair "knows" what measurement has been performed on the other, and with what outcome, even though there is no known means for such information to be communicated between the particles, which at the time of measurement may be separated by arbitrarily large distances. Einstein and others considered such behavior to be impossible, as it violated the local realist view of causality (in physics, the principle of locality states that an object is only directly influenced by its immediate surroundings; To exert an influence,

something, such as a wave or particle, must travel through the space between the two points, to carry the influence; the Special Theory of Relativity limits the speed at which all such influences can travel to the speed of light; therefore, the principle of locality implies that an event at one point cannot cause a simultaneous result at another point; in other words, information cannot travel faster than the speed of light). Einstein referred to it as "spooky action at a distance" and argued that the accepted formulation of quantum mechanics must therefore be incomplete. Later, however, the counterintuitive predictions of quantum mechanics were verified experimentally."

The 'Newtonian' worldview was proven to be wrong, yet again. The thinking of the conventional scientific field had become sclerotic and dogmatic. 'Scientific Dogma' was increasingly resembling the 'Religious Dogma' they had been in opposition to for centuries.

Every particle in the Universe is connected to every other particle, always and instantaneously. Distance is no barrier. But how is this possible?

> "Reality is an illusion, albeit a persistent one."
>
> Albert Einstein, theoretical physicist

> "The stream of knowledge is heading toward a non-mechanical reality; the universe begins to look more like a great THOUGHT than like a great machine. Mind no longer appears to be an accidental intruder into the realm of matter, we ought rather hail it as the creator and governor of the realm of matter."
>
> Sir James Hopwood Jeans, physicist (1877 – 1946)

Contemporary Physics Points to God

Robert Spitzer is the author of *New Proofs for the Existence of God*. As explained in his article titled *"How Contemporary Physics Points to God"*, a cosmological constant is a number which controls the equations of physics, and the equations of physics, in turn, describe the laws of nature. Therefore, these numbers control the laws of nature (and whether these laws of nature will be hospitable or hostile to any life form). Some examples of constants are: the speed of light constant (c= 300,000 km per second), Planck's constant ($\hbar$ = 6.6 x 10-34 joule seconds), the gravitational attraction constant (G = 6.67 x 10-11), and the strong nuclear force constant (gs = 15). Spitzer states:

> *"If the gravitational constant or weak force constant varied from their values by an exceedingly small fraction (higher or lower)—even just 0.0000000000000000000000000000000000000000000001 —then either the universe would have suffered a catastrophic collapse or would have exploded throughout its expansion, both options of which would have prevented the emergence and development of any life form."*

He goes on to say that if the gravitational constant, weak force constant, electromagnetism, or the "proton mass relative to the electron mass" ratio varied from their values by even *a tiny fraction*, the universe would have suffered a catastrophic collapse, or there would be no carbon, no hydrogen, and no *life* in the Universe. <u>The universe's fundamental constants happen to fall within the narrow range that is compatible with *life* occurring, and this simply could not have occurred by pure chance.</u>

English astronomer Fred Hoyle and American nuclear physicist William Fowler discovered the exceedingly high improbability of oxygen, carbon, helium, and beryllium having the precise values to allow for both carbon abundance and carbon bonding, which are necessary for *life*. This 'anthropic coincidence' was so striking that it caused Hoyle to abandon his previous atheism and declare: *"A common sense interpretation of the facts suggests that a super-intellect has monkeyed with physics, as well as with chemistry and biology, and that there are no blind forces worth speaking about in nature. The numbers one calculates from the facts seem to me so overwhelming as to put this conclusion almost beyond question."*

Spitzer concludes: *"The odds against all five of the anthropic coincidences happening randomly is exceedingly and almost unimaginably improbable. For this reason, many physicists attribute their occurrence to supernatural design. It is both reasonable and responsible to believe on the basis of physics, that there is a very powerful and intelligent being that caused our universe to exist as a whole. While contemporary physics does not prove the fullness of God, it certainly points to God."*

"It was not possible to formulate the laws of quantum mechanics in a fully consistent way without reference to the consciousness ... It will remain remarkable, in whatever way our future concepts may develop, that the very study of the external world led to the conclusion that the content of consciousness is the ultimate reality."

Nobel Prize winner Eugene Wigner, theoretical physicist and mathematician

"In the 1920s, the physicist Werner Heisenberg (and other founders of the science of quantum mechanics) made a discovery so strange that the world has yet to completely come to terms with it. When observing subatomic phenomena, it is impossible to completely separate the observer (that is, the scientist making the experiment) from what is being observed. In our day-to-day world, it is easy to miss this fact. We see the universe as a place full of separate objects that occasionally interact with each other, but that nonetheless remain essentially separate. On the subatomic level, however, this universe of separate objects turns out to be a complete illusion. In the realm of the super-super-small, every object in the physical universe is intimately connected with every other object. In fact, there are really no "objects" in the world at all, only vibrations of energy, and relationships. What that meant should have been obvious, though it wasn't to many. It was impossible to pursue the core reality of the universe without using consciousness. Far from being an unimportant by-product of physical processes, consciousness is not only very real – it's actually more real than the rest of physical existence, and most likely the basis of it all. But neither of these insights has yet been truly incorporated into science's picture of reality. Consciousness is the basis of all that exists."

Dr. Eben Alexander, *Proof of Heaven*

The Origin of the Universe

Stewart Swerdlow worked for over a decade at a secret underground military base in the U.S. called 'Montauk Point'. Since 'escaping' from his forced labour in that camp (he was kept there against his will because of his valuable psychic and 'remote-viewing' abilities), he has written books and lectured around the world about secret military experiments conducted at underground bases throughout the USA.

In his teachings, he describes a specific experiment that took place at Montauk Point, where subjects were injected with Sodium Pentothal ("truth serum"), LSD, and other drugs, in order to bypass their conscious minds and access *their unconscious*. By asking questions to the subjects in that state, they believed they could tap into the *global unconscious* and collect vital intelligence, perhaps even remote-view into enemy installations. The answers the scientists got about the nature of our universe were not what they expected and shocked them greatly...

In his book *'True Blood, Blue Blood'*, Stewart Swerdlow states that the following was discovered about the origin of our physical reality:

> "In the beginning, God existed as a mind and nothing else. <u>All there was, is, and ever will be, is *mind*</u>. It has no idea where It came from. It only knows that It always existed and has no end. It allows for all thought and ideas to come to fruition somewhere within Itself. It allows any and all events to occur, so in this way It knows Itself.
>
> It does not directly interfere with the personal lives of Its thought-creations. It does not have an agenda. Contrary to popular belief, It does not judge, interfere, or change anything that is already created. <u>It allows for freewill of all creations within Itself</u>. In this way, all possibilities unfold. Nothing is ever stopped from being. Humans may judge events and other beings as good or bad, positive or negative, but to the God-Mind, they are all simply pieces of Itself.
>
> The limited human mind cannot comprehend the enormity of creation."

"There are many names for this overall intelligence. It is called God, God-Mind, All That Is, Universal Mind, Cosmic Mind, Cosmic Intelligence, Hyperspace, Supreme Being, The Almighty, among other names. This initial supreme energy exists in a hyperspace state with controlling intelligence. This is a state of being that is pure energy. Here, there is instant transmission of thought and concept. The method of communication is via colour, tone, and archetype symbol. This is the foundation of all creation.

In this light, as God-Mind thought about Itself and what It was, thought forms were created that self-perpetuated in creative thought. As this energy became self-aware, all the other forms or levels began to exist simultaneously. All levels of consciousness create the levels underneath them. These thought forms created other thought forms, and so on, and so on. In this way, what is commonly referred to as Christ Consciousness and the Angelic Hierarchy were manifest.

Each manifestation, or level, is equal to every other. Where intelligence is focused gives a perspective to the consciousness. In actuality, all mind and soul-personalities exist at all levels simultaneously. However, lack of understanding and scope prevent full awareness of totality.
Eventually, a circle of creation is formed that feeds back to the original God-Mind, rather than a straight line as commonly thought. This is represented in the toroid shape.

Approximately 5 billion years ago, Angelic-like beings entered into this Milky Way galaxy and attempted to experience life in a physical universe. <u>These Angelic beings who entered in to this physical plane quickly became both physical and non-physical simultaneously.</u> [...] [Those] who stayed began remaining so long in the physical that they became trapped in the physical dimension. This is referred to as 'the fall from grace' by many traditional religions. [...] <u>Feelings of abandonment and isolation come from feeling abandoned from God Mind.</u> All problems... come from a detachment, a hurt... that your soul-personality felt from being detached and abandoned by your Creator. <u>When you realize that you ARE God-Mind, no one can have power over you. You are in control of yourself."

[…] "Physical reality is the screen or the mirror that allows us to see/reflect our own thinking. When you take responsibility for your thinking, your life gets much better. When you don't take responsibility for your thinking… it gets worse. No one is a *victim*. No one is being punished. Everyone is creating their own life. WE are creating it. If you don't like the movie that is playing… you've got to change the FILM being projected onto the screen of your life. You've got to *think differently* so that there's a different movie playing. Your Thought is the film. The brain is the *projector*. Physical reality is the screen."

Everything Is 'Mind'

What did these military experiments uncover? Ultimately, all there is… all you see around you… is just 'mind'. Thought. Pure *Consciousness*. Our Creator gets to know Itself *through us*. We were given free will, creative powers of the mind, and a physical reality in order to express ourselves, experience, learn, grow – and by doing so we are allowing *our Creator* to express Itself and experience life. We are, individually, a part of God.

Suddenly, the seemingly baffling discoveries of Quantum Physicists make sense. Physical reality is a *singular* energy field, which resembles a *thought-wave*, because we are all part of *one Consciousness*: the mind of God. Give yourself a moment to let that sink in. It was a shock for me too.

> "Quantum physicists now know that all subatomic particles such as protons, electrons, neutrons, quarks, and mesons are all actually waves. Your idea of having a solid physical body is an illusion of your senses. Your body is made up of nothing but electromagnetically resonant waves. Most of your body is empty space that contains minute fields of vibrating waves. You are a vibrating system. You are made of pure vibrating light waves, which physicists call quanta.
> [...] Think about this: If there is a Creator, what did that Being create the Universe from? There wasn't anything here before, so it must all have been created from the substance of the Creator Itself. So what are you? You are a tiny piece of the body of God."
>
> Dr. John Demartini, *The Breakthrough Experience*

Legos And How The Universe Began...

In 2005 I attended a lecture in London, and at the end of the event the speaker asked the audience if we would like to know 'How The Universe Began'. We replied in the affirmative. He stated the following:

> "In the beginning there was nothing. Then Consciousness arose. Consciousness got bored, so It created. It created, then destroyed, then created again. After a few billion years of that, Consciousness got bored again. So It created a playground. But the playground is boring, because nothing is happening on the playground. So Consciousness created a GAME. But the *game* is boring, because if you are Consciousness, you always know the outcome. It is predictable, and there's nothing at stake! For example, if you go to Las Vegas and you only bet one dollar... win a dollar or lose a dollar, so what? It's not exciting. But if you're betting your LIFE... if you believe it is a matter of life or death... if you *believe* there is the very real chance you might DIE... THEN you're going to play full out and live and experience everything to the FULLEST! One wrong turn, one wrong choice... BOOM! You're dead. Game over. But in fact... it's all part of the game! It's not 'game over'! It's 'Start Again!'
> We all know this, but we've forgotten it. Life is a game that we're here to play full out. There's never ever anything to fear. And we're all part of the same Consciousness, acting out a game."

In that moment, something 'clicked' in me. I understood a profound truth about the spiritual origin and nature of the Universe—and of *Man*. It simply... made sense.

Perhaps the penny dropped for me because as a child, I loved playing with Legos... I built entire worlds out of them. My favourite involved building space stations on a lunar surface. I would

Lego lunar surface

follow the building blueprints carefully and construct the space station. When it was built, I couldn't play anymore, so it was boring. I would tear it down and start over. I did this over and over, with the joyful abandon of a seven-year old.

And then *that* got boring. So I discarded the instructions, and I started creating new designs of my own. After a while, *that* got boring too. So I invited my friend Philippe to come play with me. It was more fun *sharing* the experience with someone outside of myself. But most of the time I played alone. So, to keep myself entertained, I used *my imagination. My creativity*. I imagined scenarios where the Lego men had all kinds of adventures: they were invading the lunar base, making plans, discussing what to do next...

It was as if a small part of my consciousness was inhabiting and animating each of these Lego men, for a brief time. Maybe they thought they were alive... but it was all... ME. I was experiencing an adventure on this imaginary lunar surface, *through them*. Perhaps because of this it wasn't a stretch for me to imagine that 'God' may be experiencing physical reality *through* us.

> "All traditions of meditation flow from one premise: that <u>the entire universe is made of one all-encompassing energy, intelligent and aware</u>, existing forever as the source of everything. Because there is nothing outside of it, say the mystics, because of its completeness, this energy has nothing to get or need, nothing to fear. The very nature of this energy, it is said, is contentment, love, peace, happiness, and perfection. The totality of this energy, say the mystics, is who you really are; your seeming separation, an illusion."
>
> Bill Harris, founder of Centerpointe Research Institute

> "I maintain that the human mystery is incredibly demeaned by scientific reductionism, with its claim in promissory materialism to account eventually for all of the spiritual world in terms of patterns of neuronal activity. This belief must be classed as a superstition... we have to recognize that we are spiritual beings with souls existing in a spiritual world as well as material beings with bodies and brains existing in a material world."
>
> Sir John C. Eccles (1903 – 1997), neurophysiologist and philosopher

Conversations With God

During a troubled and low period in his life, former radio station director Neale Donald Walsch wrote an angry letter to God asking 'why his life hadn't worked out'. A voice in his mind answered: *"Do you really want an answer to all these questions or are you just venting?"* Answers to his questions flooded into his mind and he decided to write them down. The ensuing dialogue became the book *Conversations with God*, published in 1995. Many believe this information is channelled directly from Source, though Walsch himself has stated that they are not 'channelled from God', but rather 'inspired *by* God'.

The following passage sheds more light on why God created our physical reality and echoes the revelations by Stewart Swerdlow. In answer to the question *'Where do we come from?'*, 'God' reveals the following:

> "In the beginning, that which *Is…* is all there was, and there was *nothing else.* Yet *All That Is* could not know itself – because *All That Is* is all there was, and there was nothing else. And so, *All That Is…* was not. For in the absence of something else, All That Is, is *not*.
>
> Now *All That Is knew* it was all there was – but this was not enough, **for it could only know its utter magnificence conceptually, not experientially.** Yet the *experience* of itself is that for which it longed, for it wanted to know what it *felt* like to be so magnificent. Still, this was impossible, because the very term 'magnificent' is a relative term. *All That Is* could not know what it felt like to be magnificent unless *that which is not* showed up. In the absence of that which is not, that which IS, is *not*. Do you understand this?
>
> […] The All of Everything chose to know Itself *experientially*. <u>This energy – this pure, unseen, unheard, unobserved, and therefore unknown-by-anyone-else energy – chose to experience itself as the utter magnificence It was.</u> In order to do this, It realized it would have to use a reference point *within*. It reasoned, quite correctly, that any *portion* of Itself would necessarily have to be *less than the whole*, and that if It thus simply *divided* Itself into

portions, each portion, being less than the whole, could look back on the rest of Itself and see magnificence.

And so *All That Is* divided Itself – becoming, in one glorious moment, that which is this, that which is that. For the first time, *this* and *that* existed, quite apart from each other. And still, both existed simultaneously. As did all that was *neither*.

Thus, three elements suddenly existed: that which is *here*. That which is *there* and that which is neither here nor there – but which *must exist* for *here* and *there* to exist. [...] Those who believe that God is All That Is *and* All That Is Not, are those whose understanding is correct.

Now in creating that which is "here" and that which is "there," God made it possible for God to know Itself. **In the moment of this great explosion from within**, God created relativity – the greatest gift God ever gave to Itself. Thus, relationship is the greatest gift God ever gave to you.

[Thoughts are energy. Thoughts have a vibrational frequency. Physical matter is condensed 'thought energy'. Consciousness started vibrating on itself at such speed that the resulting explosion created all the physical matter in the Universe: an event known as 'The Big Bang'...]

From the No-Thing thus sprang the Everything – a spiritual event entirely consistent, incidentally, with what your scientists call The Big Bang Theory.

As the elements of all raced forth, *time* was created, for a thing was first *here*, then it was *there* – and the period it took to get from here to there was measurable.

Just as the parts of Itself which are seen began to define themselves, 'relative' to each other, so, too, did the parts which are unseen. God knew that for love to exist – and to know itself as *pure love* – its exact opposite had to exist as well. So God voluntarily created the great polarity – the absolute opposite of love – everything that love is not – what is now called fear. In the moment fear existed, love could exist *as a thing that could be experienced*.

[...] In other words, not only was the physical universe thus created, but the metaphysical universe as well. The part of God which forms the second half of the Am/Not Am equation also exploded into an infinite number of units smaller than the whole. These energy units you would call spirits.

[…] **My divine purpose in dividing Me was to create sufficient parts of Me so that I could know Myself experientially.** There is only one way for the Creator to know Itself experientially as the Creator, and that is to create. And so I gave to each of the countless parts of Me (to all of My spirit children) the *same power to create* which I have as the whole.

This is what your religions mean when they say that you were created in the 'image and likeness of God'. This doesn't mean that our physical bodies look alike. It does mean that our essence is the same. We are composed of the same stuff. We ARE the 'same stuff'! With all the same properties and abilities – including the ability to create physical reality out of thin air."

According to the passage above, all the 'physical' matter in the Universe is condensed 'thought energy' from our Creator – it comes from the mind of God. Human beings' bodies and souls are a small part of *the whole*. We are all *one* and we have the same creative powers as our Creator. We can use our amazing mind power to 'create our world' and change our life (more on this in *Part III*).

> "Science has told us that we are outside of our Universe, that we're alone, that we're separate. […] We're now realizing that that paradigm is wrong, that we aren't separate. We are all one. We are all together. Quantum Mechanics, the 'New Physics' has been affirming what Eastern mystics have been saying for centuries: that we are all connected. This view of separateness is one of the most destructive things. It's the thing that creates ALL the problems in the world. And we're now realizing that that paradigm is wrong. We aren't separate. We are all one. We are all together. And so we are trying to understand and absorb what are the implications to that. What does this really mean to me and to my life?"
>
> Lynne McTaggart, author of *"The Field"*

The Universe is a Mental Construct

How can our solid world be made up of atoms, and yet we know that atoms are not solid? There is no contradiction if you understand that we are all part of a singular *Consciousness*. We are living in the Mind of God... *Atoms are not creating a solid world because the world isn't solid. It is a mental construct.*

Our physical reality is merely an illusion; a theatre stage; *All the world's a stage, and all the men and women merely players*, as Shakespeare put it. This virtual reality we inhabit allows us to play out the game called 'life', <u>for the purpose of self-expression and spiritual progress</u>.

Science will make great leaps forward when it finally marries its methods to spirituality. Science must recognize that there is *consciousness* in everything. Everything we are working with is part of a unified *intelligence*. If science keeps removing itself from spirituality it will keep creating more problems for humanity, and keep making us feel lost, desperate for answers. Science will not progress until *Consciousness* is factored into the equation.

> "The day science begins to study non-physical phenomena, it will make more progress in one decade than in all the previous centuries of its existence. To understand the true nature of the universe, one must think it terms of energy, frequency and vibration."
>
> Nikola Tesla

How This Knowledge Changed My Life

For many years I felt isolated and depressed. I stayed away from other people. But ever since I recognized that separation between us humans is an illusion (because we are all 'ONE'), I was able to walk into a supermarket, the subway, or a crowded street and *feel connected to everyone*.

I also began to appreciate every moment of my life as an incredible adventure, something to savour; the most exquisite GIFT ever. I saw divinity in everything. A perfect plan unfolding before my very eyes.

I was able to feel love and acceptance, for myself in a first instance, and then for others. I was able to start speaking to crowds of 1,000+ people because I no longer felt afraid of being judged or of 'what other people think'. Since we are all one, how could a part of me... judge... me? That would me ridiculous, no? Love is the only rational feeling towards another part of *you*. And by healing a part of *you*, do you not heal yourself? By helping a part of *you*, are you not helping *yourself*?

* * * * *

Where do we come from? Scientists and mystics have arrived to the same conclusion, as incredible as it may seem.

We come from the mind of God.

CHAPTER 2

What Happens After We Die?

Thousands of people have died, been resuscitated through medical means, and told us *exactly* what they experienced 'on the other side'. Thousands more have described their time *in between lives* – in the spirit world – under hypnosis, in the context of past-life regression therapy. Many more people have had profound spiritual experiences and 'out-of-body' experiences, connecting briefly with the spirit world. Military insiders have leaked *what the army knows* about life after death, from secret experiments conducted on the human unconscious. Psychics and channellers—people with extra-sensory perceptions, able to communicate with the spirit world—are yet another source of information about the spirit world.

All these sources of information tell us *the same thing*:

- We are part of a Creator or 'Source' (God-Mind)
- There *is* a spirit world.
- Our soul is in constant contact with our *spirit guide* present in this spirit world. We are never alone.
- We reincarnate, in order to experience physical reality and express ourselves. *Life is a gift*.
- We are all connected.
- Love is all that truly matters.
- Death is merely an illusion, a doorway to us going 'home'.

As I mentioned at the beginning of this book, psychologist Raymond Moody's subjects stated, after visiting the spirit world:

- ❑ *"Life is forever. Death is nothing more than a doorway. Something that you walk through... Death is a railroad station where you come, always, to go to another life. We cannot die because we are already created... to live forever."*

- ❑ *"In the spirit world you feel an overwhelming feeling of love and acceptance. I would exchange twenty lifetimes for a few moments in the presence of that love and acceptance... <u>You are so deeply loved and you yourself so deeply love</u>. Love is what keeps this world alive. We are alive because of love."*

- ❑ *"When you return to the spirit world from whence you came, you begin to sense a part of yourself greater and far more magnificent than you ever give yourself credit for. <u>You are a part of All That Is, and so is everyone else</u>. As a result, you become a lot more understanding of others."*

- ❑ *"Upon returning to the spirit world you are asked: How did you learn to love and accept your fellow humans in the way Source totally accepts and loves you?"*

In this chapter we will explore the reality of life after death in more detail through the fascinating out-of-body case studies of Dr. Eben Alexander and Anita Moorjani, as well as a dozen case studies from past-life regression therapist Michael Newton. Their stories are pregnant with meaning. They also offer up compelling proof to the existence of 'God'.

According to a report by the International Association for Near-Death Studies (IANDS) in 2007, based on 787 near-death experience reports:

- ❑ 67.7% report an out-of-body experience
- ❑ Almost as many report seeing a light at the end of a tunnel.
- ❑ Almost 50% report seeing unearthly beings.
- ❑ 21.6% report experiencing a life review.
- ❑ More than 50% report strong emotional tone and receiving knowledge.
- ❑ 71.4% of the women developed healing or psychic abilities after their near-death experience. 60.7% of the men developed healing or psychic abilities after their near-death experience.

Dr. Eben Alexander's Near-Death Experience

Eben Alexander is a neurosurgeon, and the author of *Proof of Heaven*. An illness led to him being in a coma for a few months, during which time he was declared 'brain-dead'. Miraculously, he recovered. He writes the following about his out-of-body experience and the wisdom his spirit guide shared with him while his consciousness was in the spirit world:

"Without using any words, she spoke to me. The message had three parts: "You are loved and cherished, dearly, forever. You have nothing to fear. There is nothing you can do wrong." If I had to boil it to one sentence: You are loved. And, to just one word: Love.

Love is, without a doubt, the basis of everything. This is the reality of realities, the incomprehensibly glorious truth of truths that lives and breathes at the core of everything that exists or that ever will exist. The message flooded me with a vast and crazy sensation of relief. It was like being handed the rules to a game I'd been playing all my life without ever fully understanding it."

"My situation was akin to that of a foetus in a womb. In this case, the "mother" was God, the Creator, the Source who is responsible for making the universe and all in it. This Being was so close that there seemed to be no distance at all between God and myself. Yet at the same time, I could sense the infinite vastness of the Creator, could see how completely minuscule I was by comparison. 'Om' was the sound I remembered hearing associated with that omniscient, omnipotent, and unconditionally loving God, but any descriptive word falls short. [...]

Through the Orb, Om told me that there is not one universe but many —in fact, more than I could conceive— but that love lay at the center of them all. Evil was present in all the other universes as well, but only in the tiniest trace amounts. Evil was necessary because without it free will was impossible, and without free will there could be no growth, no forward movement, no chance for us to become what God longed for us to be. ...in the larger picture love was overwhelmingly dominant, and it would ultimately be triumphant. Small particles of evil were scattered throughout the universe, but the sum total of all that evil was as a grain of sand on a vast beach compared to the goodness, abundance, and unconditional love in which the universe was literally awash."

"*The universe has no beginning or end, and God is entirely present within every particle of it... It was as if, just as no physical particle in the universe is really separate from another, so in the same way there was no such thing as a question without an accompanying answer. [...] The physical side of the universe is as a speck of dust compared to the invisible, spiritual part.*"

"*My experience showed me that the death of the body and the brain are not the end of consciousness, that human experience continues beyond the grave. More important, it continues under the gaze of a God who loves and cares about each one of us... The place I went was real. Real in a way that makes the life we're living here and now completely dreamlike by comparison.*"

"*One by one I ran down the suggestions that I knew my colleagues, and I myself in the old days, would have offered to "explain" what happened to me. [...] The more I read of the "scientific" explanations of what NDEs are, the more I was shocked by their transparent flimsiness.*"

"*Modern neuroscience dictates that the brain gives rise to consciousness... Sure, scientists hadn't discovered exactly how the neurons of the brain managed to do this... [In reality] the brain doesn't produce consciousness. It is, instead, a kind of reducing valve or filter, shifting the larger, nonphysical consciousness that we possess into a more limited capacity for the duration of our mortal lives. Forgetting our trans-earthly identities allows us to be "here and now". [...] From a more purpose-focused perspective, making the right decision through our free will in the face of the evil and injustice on earth would mean far less if we remembered, while here, the full beauty and brilliance of what awaits us. [...] To say that there is still a chasm between our current scientific understanding of the universe and the truth as I saw it is a considerable understatement.*"

"*For all of the successes of Western civilization, the world has paid a dear price in terms of the most crucial component of existence – our human spirit.*"

> "One of the biggest myths of humankind is the subject of death. It provokes perceptions of fear, pain, and suffering on Earth, yet it is simply another illusion. We're not mortal beings having occasional spiritual experiences. We are immortal beings having a brief mortal experience. That's the actual truth hidden behind all of our mortal perceptions."
>
> Dr. John Demartini, *The Breakthrough Experience*

Anita Moorjani's Near-Death Experience

Anita Moorjani is the author of *Dying To Be Me*. In 2002 she was diagnosed with cancer, and, after four years of struggling with the disease—having developed large tumours throughout her body—her organs began to fail. She slipped into a coma, and doctors gave her just hours to live.

As her body lay there dying, Anita had an out-of-body-experience. In this state, Anita experienced profound peace and love. She also learned about the laws of life, including how she had caused her own cancer. She was then given the choice of remaining in the spirit world, or return to Earth. She was told that her body would heal itself if she returned. Anita awoke from her coma and within *days* her body was fully healed. Her doctors were at a loss to explain this miracle.

She writes the following of her near-death experience:

> "I felt free, liberated, and magnificent! Every pain, ache, sadness, and sorrow was gone. …<u>I then had a sense of being encompassed by something that I can only describe as pure, unconditional love</u>, but even the word *love* doesn't do it justice … I felt completely bathed and renewed in this energy, and it made me feel as though I *belonged*… I had finally come home … the combination of a sense of joy mixed with a generous sprinkling of jubilation and happiness. … It didn't feel as though I'd *physically* gone somewhere else—it was more as though I'd *awakened*. … My soul was finally realizing its true magnificence! […] I suddenly *knew* things that weren't physically possible, such as the conversations between medical staff and my family that were taking place far away from my hospital bed. […] To my amazement, I became aware of the presence of my father, who'd died ten years earlier, and it brought me an unbelievable level of comfort to sense him with me. …I was also aware of other beings around me. I didn't recognize them, but I knew they loved me very much and were protecting me."

Anita had not been close to her father, while he was alive, but in this moment, she only felt unconditional love emanating from him. And he reminded her of this important spiritual truth:

> *"Dad, it feels like I've come home! I'm so glad to be here. Life is so painful!* I told him. *But you're always home, darling,* he impressed upon me. *You always were, and you always will be. I want you to remember that."*

The souls of her father and her recently-deceased friend Soni urged her to return to her body, with this message: *"Now that you know the truth of who you really are, go back and live your life <u>fearlessly</u>!"*

When she awoke in her body, she astounded her doctors and her loved ones by recounting their conversations in other parts of the hospital, and even more so by becoming cancer-free *within days*. She explains that her miraculous recovery was due to retuning to 'a state of love':

> "The question I get asked most frequently when sharing my story is: *So, what caused your cancer?* I can sum up the answer in one word: *fear*. What was I afraid of? Just about everything, including failing, being disliked, letting people down, and not being good enough. I was a people pleaser and feared disapproval, regardless of the source. I bent over backward to avoid people thinking ill of me; and over the years, I lost myself in the process. I was completely disconnected from who I was or what I wanted, because everything I did was designed to win approval. [...] I understood that the cancer wasn't a punishment or anything like that. It was just my own energy, manifesting as cancer because my fears weren't allowing me to express myself as the magnificent force I was meant to be.
>
> [...] Why, oh why, have I always been so harsh with myself? Why was I always beating myself up? Why was I always forsaking myself? Why did I never stand up for myself and show the world the beauty of my own soul? Why was I always suppressing my own intelligence and creativity to please others? I betrayed myself every time I said yes when I meant no! Why have I violated myself by always needing to seek approval from others just to be myself? Why haven't I followed my own beautiful heart and spoken my own truth? How come I never knew that we're not supposed to be so tough on ourselves?

[…] There was nobody punishing me. I finally understood that it was *me* I hadn't forgiven, not other people. *I was the one who was judging me, whom I'd forsaken, and whom I didn't love enough.* […] I saw myself as a beautiful child of the universe. Just the fact that I existed made deserving of unconditional love. I realized that I didn't need to *do* anything to deserve this. …I'm loved unconditionally, for no other reason than simply because I exist … I saw that I'd never loved myself, valued myself, or seen the beauty of my own soul. …*we already are what we spend our lives trying to attain,* but we just don't realize it!

[…] <u>I understood that my body is only a reflection of my internal state. If my inner self were aware of its greatness and connection with All-that-is, my body would soon reflect that and heal rapidly</u>."

This experience had a profound impact on Anita's life, as one can imagine. After leaving the hospital, her outlook on life had transformed. She states:

"I danced and drank champagne gleefully. <u>I knew more than ever that life was to be lived with joy and abandon</u>. … I saw divinity in everything—every animal and insect. I developed a much greater interest in the natural world than I had before. … Every day was a fresh adventure. I wanted to walk, drive, explore, sit on the hills and the sand, and just take in this life! … I was awed by it all. The deliciousness of each day made me feel as though I'd just been born. […] <u>I feel that people have lost the ability to see the magic of life. They didn't share my wonder or enthusiasm for my surroundings</u>—and just being alive. They seemed caught up in routine, and their minds were on the next thing they had to do. …they've forgotten how to just be in the moment."

Is it any surprise so many people feel anxious, afraid, depressed, and lost, when they are disconnected from such truth and beauty? *When they are ignoring their very essence?*

Michael Newton's *Journey of Souls*

The hypnotherapist Michael Newton – author of the book *Journey of Souls* – helped thousands of people overcome traumatic experiences through the use of hypnosis, and inspired millions of people around the world with his remarkable books. He recently passed away, at the age of 84.

Past life regression therapy, he explains, begins with regressing the subject to their earliest memory as a child: *"In your mind, go back to when you were three years old... two years old... one year old... in the womb of your mother... move back in time to your previous life... Now, move forward to the moment of your passing...".* During these sessions, after putting his patient under deep hypnosis, he was able to speak directly to their unconscious mind, asking them questions about their past lives. Their responses would challenge his previously-held atheistic views. I share twelve of his case studies, below.

His clients reported that the first moments after dying can feel a bit strange, and jarring. But there is also an indescribable feeling of relief, love, freedom, and weightlessness. Often the soul tries to console, mentally, its loved ones still in physical reality. Three case studies at the beginning of Michael Newton's book describe the initial moments after death:

> *"I'm rising up higher... still floating... looking back at my body. It's like watching a movie, only I'm in it! The doctor is comforting my wife and daughter. My wife is sobbing. I'm trying to reach into her mind... to tell her everything is all right with me. She is so overcome by grief I'm not getting through. I want her to know my suffering is gone... I'm free of my body... I don't need it any more... that I will wait for her. I want her to know that... Oh, I'm moving away now..."*

> *"[I feel] like... a force... of some kind... pushing me up out of my body. I'm ejected out the top of my head. [I'm radiating light] from... my energy. I look sort of transparent white... my soul... A wispy... string... hanging... It's wonderful to feel so free with no more pain, but... I am...*

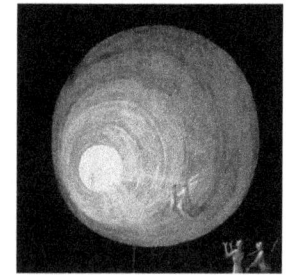

Hieronymus Bosch, *Ascent of the Blessed*

disoriented... I didn't expect to die... It's strange... it's as if I'm suspended in air that isn't air... there are no limits... no gravity... I'm weightless. I can [control some of my movements] but there is... a pulling... into a bright whiteness... it's so bright! [...] A kind of magnetic... force... but... I want to stay a little longer... I'm over Will's head. I'm trying to console him. I want him to feel my love is not really gone... I want him to know he has not lost me forever and that I will see him again... I know I'm dead... but I'm not ready to leave Will yet... [...] It's time for me to go... they are coming for me now... I'm moving... into a brighter light."

"The tunnel is a hollow, dim vent... and there is a small circle of light at the other end. I feel a tugging... a gentle pulling... I'm supposed to drift through this tunnel... and I do... I'm being summoned forward. The circle of light grows very wide and... I'm out of the tunnel. There is a ... cloudy brightness... a light fog. I'm filtering through it... It's so still... it is such a quiet place to be in... I am in the place of spirits... [...] Thought! I feel the power of thought all around me. I feel... thoughts of love... companionship... empathy... and it's all combined with... anticipation... as if others are... waiting for me. I feel secure... I'm aware of thoughts reaching out to me... of caring... nurturing. It is strange, but there is also the understanding around me of just who I am and why I am here now... I sense it – a harmony of thought everywhere."

* * * * *

Newton goes on to share more remarkable reports from the after-life, as described by his clients. The subject in the case study below is remembering a life as a man who committed suicide in the early 1900s. He is worried about having to meet his spirit guide. While there is no such thing as 'Hell' or 'eternal damnation' in the afterlife (contrary to religious teachings might say), he hasn't exactly covered himself in glory. Also, he will have to re-live the pain and despair that led to his suicide in his *next* reincarnation... If you don't face up to your problems in this lifetime, and learn to overcome them, they are only going to keep coming back again and again, lifetime after lifetime, until you do. The subject, under hypnosis, states:

"I am going to see my advisor [spirit guide]... his name is Clodees... I am going to have to make some kind of... accounting... of myself. We go through this after all my lives, but this time I'm really in the soup [because I

killed myself]. [...] <u>There is no such thing here as punishment – that's an Earth condition</u>. Clodees will be disappointed that I bailed out early and didn't have the courage to face my difficulties. By choosing to die as I did means I have to come back later and deal with the same thing all over again in a different life. I just wasted a lot of time by checking out early. ...My friends won't give me any pats on the back either – I feel sadness at what I did. [...] I blew it! I have to see him to explain why things didn't work out. [...] You know, if it weren't for Earth's beauty – the birds, flowers, trees – I would never go back. It's too much trouble."

The subject in the next case study is describing how, after being greeted by his spirit guide and loved ones, he is moved on to some sort of 'staging area', before being transported to his spiritual 'home'. Once there, there is a time to reflect on the lessons from the life the subject has just experienced. Sometimes, they are given glimpses of future possibilities.

"Once I have arrived in the spiritual space where I belong, I go to school with my friends, where we study... My teacher [comes to meet me]. She takes me inside my temple school. I see a large library. Small gatherings of people are speaking in quiet tones... at tables... it is sedate... warm... a secure feeling which is familiar to me. My friends (about twenty) immediately greet me. Oh, it's so good to be back. I can't tell you how happy I am to be with them once more. We are all close – I've known them for ages. [...] I go to my table and we all look at the life books. They are multi-dimensional. They shift... from a center of... crystal... which changes with reflected light. The pictures are alive. We can see... in miniature... our past lives and the alternatives... I see a lack of self-discipline in my last life because this is what is on my mind. I see myself dying young, in a lover's quarrel – my ending was useless. [...] We can look at future possibilities... in small bites only... in the form of lessons... We all help one another go over our mistakes during this cycle. We do a lot of studying together and discuss the value of our choices."

* * * * *

The subject in the following case study, confirms how our physical reality is merely an illusion – a stage, designed for us to experience life. Showing courage, bravery, and love for our fellow human beings is what is prized most in the afterlife... The patient stated, under hypnosis:

"My old friends are around me and we are talking about the foolishness of life. We rib each other about how dramatic it all is down there on Earth and how seriously we all take our lives. <u>Earth is one big stage play — we all know that. We see ourselves as actors in a gigantic stage production.</u> [...] We live life to its fullest because we are talented at taking what life has to offer.

[...] Dubri [a member of my soul family] did one outstanding thing. Once, during heavy seas, a sailor fell off the mast into the ocean and was drowning. Dubri tied a line around his waist and dove off the deck. He risked his life and saved a shipmate. We praised him for what he did with admiration in our minds. We came to the same conclusion that none of us could match this single act of courage in our last lives.

[...] Regrets... I feel sorry if I have hurt someone... But we learn. We talk among ourselves... and try to make amends the next time. [...] We want to be recognized by one another for being sincere in working on our individual programs. [...] (zestfully) Every time I leave for a new role on Earth, I say goodbye with, 'See you all back here A.D. (after death)!"

* * * * *

Everything serves us. There are spiritual reasons behind even the most tragic and sorrowful events in our lives. In the following case study, the subject explains that prior to reincarnating into his previous life, his spirit guide Idis assigned him the task of taking care of his disabled brother:

"I'm taking care of my brother Billy. His face and hands were horribly burned by a flash fire from a kitchen stove when he was four years old. I was ten when it happened. I'm a woman in Canada. I'm Billy's sister. My mother and brother require someone mentally tough to hold the family together and give them a course to follow. I'm a baker and I'll never marry, because I can't leave them. [My brother's major lesson is] to acquire humility without being crushed by a life of little self-gratification. [...] Idis [my spirit guide] and I had discussed the whole situation. She said Billy's soul would require a caretaker. [...] The degree of difficulty in a life is measured by how challenging the situation is for you, not others. For me, being Billy's caretaker is harder than when I was on the receiving end with another soul as my caretaker. [The most difficult factor of this assignment for me as a caretaker was] to sustain a child... through their helplessness... to adulthood... to teach a child to confront torment with courage. <u>Without

> *addressing and overcoming pain you can never really connect with who you are and build on that. I must tell you, the more pain and adversity which come to you as a child, the more opportunity to expand your potential."*

This case study reminds me that there is divine perfection, love, and balance even in the most horrible and seemingly unfair situations. We are not victims.

* * * * *

The subject in the next case study states that we are all part of a singular Creator or "Maker". This subject, an 'advanced' soul who has experienced many reincarnations, mentions that part of her role while in physical reality is to assist others to *"express true benevolence through their passion."*

> *"We are... as particles... of energized units. We originated out of one unit. The maker. [...] Part of us never leaves, since we do not totally separate from the maker. The part that remains in the spirit wold... is... more dormant... waiting to be rejoined to the rest of our energy. [...] We get kudos for doing well on the hard worlds. [...] What really appeals to me about Earth... the kinship humans have for each other while they struggle against one another... competing and collaborating at the same time. That contradiction is what appeals to me – mediating quarrels of a fallible race which has so much pride and need of self-respect. The human brain is rather unique, you know. Humans are egocentric but vulnerable. They can make their character mean and yet have a great capacity for kindness. There is weak and courageous behaviour on Earth. It's always a push-me pull-you tug-of-war going on with human values. This diversity suits my soul. [...] Those of us developing on Earth have... a sanction to help humans know of the infinite beyond their life and to assist them in expressing true benevolence through their passion. Having a passion to fight for life – that's what is so worthwhile about humanity. [...] When humans experience trouble, they can be at their best and are... quite noble."*

* * * * *

In the next case study, the subject explains how, prior to reincarnating, a soul chooses a new life to experience in physical reality, by using a tool described as 'The Ring of Destiny'. This is reminiscent of choosing which character or avatar you want to play in a modern-day video game!

"A soft voice comes into my mind and says, "It's about time, don't you think?" It's my instructor. Some of us have to be given a push when they think we are ready again. I'd like to stay... but the instructors don't want us hanging around here too long or we will get into a rut. I'm excited about this. <u>I would have no satisfaction without my physical lives</u>.

I have made the decision I want to come back to Earth. When my trainer and I agree the time is right to accomplish things, I send out thoughts... my messages are received by the coordinators, who actually assist us in previewing our life possibilities at the Ring of Destiny. [...] I am floating towards the Ring... it's circular... a monster bubble. The Ring is surrounded by banks of screens... [...] I am hovering the middle, watching the panorama of life all around me... places... people... cities... I'm going to mentally operate the panel, a mass of lights and buttons. [...] I am traveling through time now on the lines and watching the images on the screens change. I'm scanning. The stops are major turning points on life's pathways involving important decisions... possibilities.... Events which make it necessary to consider alternate choices in time."

"Oh, there is destiny, alright. The life cycles are in place. It's just that there are so many alternatives which are unclear. [...] The controllers... come into my mind to see if I am satisfied with what I have been shown. I go back to talk to my companions before making up my mind."

* * * * *

The subject in the following case study had a lifetime of pain just above her knees. Doctors couldn't find anything wrong with her. In this session, while under hypnosis, she describes a life as a six-year-old girl named Ashley, living in New England in 1871. She was riding in a fully loaded, horse-drawn carriage when suddenly the door opened and she tumbled out of the vehicle. When she hit the cobble-stone street, one of the heavy rear carriage wheels rolled over her legs, above both knees, crushing the bones. After a productive period of years as a writer and tutor of disadvantaged children, Ashley died in 1912, at the age of 41. The subject explains that some 1000 years earlier, she had chosen to be one of the strongest physical specimens on Earth, in the body of a powerful Viking named Leth. This choice needed to be balanced, which is why her soul chose to experience life as Ashley, a crippled girl, in the late 1800s. She stated, under hypnosis:

"I chose to be crippled to gain intellectual concentration. Being unable to walk made me read and study more. I developed my mind... and listened to my mind... I learned to communicate well and to write with skill because I wasn't distracted. I was always in bed. [...] I chose this family because they needed the intensity of love with someone totally dependent upon them all their lives. We were very close as a family because they were lonely before I was born. I came late, as their only child. They wanted a daughter who would not marry and leave them to be lonely again."

"When I saw Ashley for the first time... I was able to see her without me... healthy... older... another life possibility... I saw a grown woman... normal legs... unhappiness with a man... frustration at being trapped in an unrewarding life... sorrowful parents... but easier. No! That course would not have worked well for either of us – I was the best soul for her."

"[...] She was being naughty, bouncing around in the carriage, playing with the door handle when her mother said she must stop. Then... I was ready and she was ready...

[...] The agony of those first five weeks was beyond belief. I almost died, but I learned from enduring it all. [In my current life] I benefit every day by my appreciation of the necessity of a union between mind and body to learn lessons."

Following this past-life regression the subject no longer experienced pain above her knees. She had come to terms with what had happened to her, with love, compassion, and understanding.

> *"Souls search for self-expression by developing different aspects of their character. Regardless of what physical or mental tools are used through the use of many bodies, the laws of karma will prevail. If the soul chooses one extreme, somewhere down the line this will be counterbalanced by an opposite choice to even-out development. The physical lives of Leth the powerful Viking and Ashley [crippled at six years old] are examples of karmic compensation. The Hindus believe a rich man sooner or later must become a beggar for his soul to develop adequately."*
>
> Michael Newton, *"Journey of Souls"*

Chapter 2: What Happens After We Die?

Spiritual Origins Of Life

Michael Newton writes: "Souls are given the opportunity to participate in the development of lower forms of intelligent life in order to advance themselves." During a past-life regression with an 'advanced soul', the subject, under hypnosis, revealed the following about how certain life forms are created on certain worlds, using the creative power of the mind:

M.N: *"Does your energy utilize the properties of light, heat, and motion in the creation of life?"*

Subject: *"I am proficient with fish. We start with the embryos. We give instructions to... organisms... within the surrounding conditions.... I'm working in oceans.... I started with basic sea life such as algae and plankton... we begin with microorganisms... small cells, and this is very difficult to learn. The cells of life... our energy cannot become proficient unless we can direct it to... alter molecules.*
We must learn to be able to split cells and give DNA instructions by sending particles of energy into protoplasm. We must learn to do this... coordinating it with a sun's energy, because each sun has different energy effects on the worlds around them. We examine new structures... mutations.... To watch and see what is workable. We arrange substances for their most effective use with different suns. [...] Usually a planet hospitable to life has souls watching and whatever we do is natural. [...] We must learn to work together to combine our energy for the best results."

M.N: *"Who does the full-sized thermonuclear explosions which create physical universes and space itself?"*

Subject: *"The source... the concentrated energy of the Old Ones."*

Michael Newton, *Journey of Souls*

* * * * *

In the next case study, the subject describes attending a 'recognition class' prior to being reincarnated into his present life.

"I must go to recognition class. It's an observation meeting... with my companions... so I can recognize them later. I see a circular auditorium with a raised dais in the middle – that's where the speakers are. There are about ten or fifteen souls around me... people who are going to be close to me in the life to come. I have to hear what the speakers are saying. They are the prompters. They give us the signs by coming up with ingenious ideas, so we will know what to look for in our next life. <u>The signs are placed in our mind now in order to jog our memories later as humans. Signs, flags... – markers in the road of life. They kick us into a new direction in life at certain times when something important is supposed to happen</u>... and then we must know the signs to recognize one another too.

My primary soulmate is here... and there are other people that I am supposed to contact... the others need their signs too. After this class we usually don't forget the important signs." [...] "The most important recognition sign I must remember from this class... Melinda's laugh.
[...] Leaving Clair was hard... We were sexually attracted to each other in high school. The infatuation had no real mental connection... it's so hard on Earth to figure out what you are supposed to do with other people... sex is a big trap... we would have grown bored with one another."
[...] I can see it all now. Our tutor was helping Melinda and me that night. My idea to go to the dance was sudden. I hate to dance because I'm clumsy. I didn't know anybody in the town yet and felt stupid, but I was guided there. When I saw her at the dance, alarms went off. I did something very uncharacteristic of me... I cut in on the man she was dancing with. When I first held her my legs were like rubber. We felt as if we were in another world... there was this familiarity... it was so weird during that dance... a knowing without doubt that something important was unfolding... the guidance... the intent of our meeting... our hearts were racing... it was enchantment." [...] Clair was in my life earlier to tempt me to stay on the farm... one of the false trails I needed to get past... another kind of life. After I left, Clair found the right person. [...] It would not have been as good [with Clair]. There is one main course of life we choose in advance, but alternatives always exist and we learn from them too. [...]

There are times in my lives when I change directions because of too much thinking and analysis. Or, I do nothing for the same reasons."

* * * * *

> ### The Act Of Conjunction
>
> Michael Newton: *"You said the ultimate objective of souls was to seek unification with the supreme source of creative energy."*
>
> Subject: *"The act of conjunction, yes."*
>
> M.N: *"Does the source dwell in some special central space in the spirit world?"*
>
> Subject: *"The source is the spirit world."*
>
> *"It's as if we are all part of a universal train on a flat track of existence. Most of the souls on Earth are in one car moving along the track."*
>
> M.N: *"Where is the engine?"*
>
> Subject: *"The maker? Up front, naturally."*
>
> M.N: *"It would be nice if all of us were closer to the engine."*
>
> Subject: *"Ultimately, we will be."*
>
> Michael Newton, *Journey of Souls*

* * * * *

The subject in the following case study is a businessman by the name of 'Steve', who owns a successful clothing firm in Texas. He has had two failed marriages and he is an alcoholic. Michael Newton writes: *"His mother disappeared after leaving him on the steps of a church in Texas within a week of his birth. After a few lonely and unhappy years in an orphanage, an older couple adopted him, stern disciplinarians who seemed to disapprove of him all the time. Steve left home in his teens, had many scrapes with the law, and once attempted suicide. His anger was rooted in feelings of isolation and abandonment issues."*

This case study delves into the consequences of the deliberate severing of a child/parent bond:

> *"I'm in a basket... there is a faded blue blanket around me... I'm being set down on some steps... it's cold... My mother... is bending down over me... saying goodbye... (begins to cry)... She is young... not married to my father... he is already married. She is... crying... I can feel her tears falling on my face... I see flowing back hair... beautiful... I reach up and touch her mouth... she kisses me... soft, gentle... she is having a terribly hard time leaving me here. (subject can hardly talk) She says: "I must leave you for your own good. I have no money to take care of you. My parents won't help us. I love you. I will always love you and hold you in my heart forever." She... takes hold of a heavy door knocker... and bangs on the door... we hear footsteps coming... now she is gone. (almost overcome by emotion) Oh... she wanted me after all... she didn't want to leave me... she loved me!"*

Newton then asks his client if he remembers *another* lifetime with his mother. Steve answers:

> *"Yes... I have [lived in another life with the soul of my birth mother]. I'm standing in front of my temple... before a large crowd of people... my guards are in the back of me. My name is Haroum. I am wearing a long, white robe and sandals. I have a staff in my hand with gold snakes on it as a symbol of my authority. I am a high priest [a tribal leader located on the Arabian Peninsula close to the Red Sea around 2000 BC, in what was known as the Kingdom of Sheba]. I am on the steps judging a woman. She is my mother. She is kneeling down in front of me. There is a look of pity and fear in her eyes as she looks up at me. There is pity in her eyes because of the power which has consumed me... in taking so much control over the daily lives of my people. And there is fear, too, for what I am about to do. This disturbs me, but I must not show it."*

> *"She has broken into the storage house and stolen food to give to the people. Many are hungry at this time of year, but I alone can order distribution. The food must be measured out carefully. [...] By disobeying me she is undermining my authority. I use the distribution of food as a means of... control over my people. I want them all to be loyal to me. [...] My mother has violated the law. I can save her, but she must be punished as an example. I decide she will die. [...] It must be done. She has been a constant thorn in my side – causing unrest among my people because of her position. I cannot govern freely with her here any longer. Even now, she is defiant. I order her*

death by banging my staff on the stone steps. [...] I must not think about such things [sadness about ordering his mother's execution] if I am to maintain power."

"I was sent to the place where we look at lives [The Ring of Destiny]. I talk about this guy Steve who is so unhappy... no real mother... all that stuff... what kinds of people will be around him... their plans, too... it must fit all together for us. We need to firm that up. No one is forced to do anything. We know what should be done. Jor [my spirit guide]... and the others help us make adjustments... they are sent in to round out the picture... [...] It's... Eone [the souls of my mother]... she wants to be... my mother again. [She] is telling me it's time for us to settle things... to be in a disordered life as mother and son again. [...] I just wasn't ready to offset the harm I did her as Haroum. She says the circumstances are right for this exercise now."

"My life as Steve is not supposed to be punishment. [...] <u>The lesson to be learned... to feel what desertion is like in a family relationship... deliberate severing</u>... The severing of the mother and son bond by deliberate action... to appreciate what it is like to be cast off."

"Talu and Kalish [the souls of my adoptive parents] are so hard for me to be with... [...] They are going to make a lot of demands on me as a child, Kalish sarcastic, Talu a perfectionist, losing Eone... it's going to be a rough ride."

"We (the soul) don't control the human mind... we try by our presence to... elevate it to see... meaning in the world and to be receptive to morality... to give understanding."

"[I accepted Steve's body] to... rise above my attraction for leading others... always wanting to be in charge. My weakness is... using power for self-preservation on Earth. [...] My adoptive parents were rough on me... [for me] to know what being constantly judged is like... and to overcome... and be whole."

This story, above, really puts into perspective the perceived injustices we believe we have experienced during our childhood. Could it be that we actually *chose* our family and the circumstances of our birth? Could it be that we *chose* to be abandoned at birth for reasons only known to our soul?

In this final case study from the book *Journey of Souls*, the subject is describing the process of reincarnation, leaving the spirit world to re-enter physical reality. According to this subject, under hypnosis, it requires a time of adjustment, to 'meld' with the body and brain of a human baby. The soul of the subject has chosen its future parents and its future incarnation in the Ring of Destiny. Agreements ('compacts') are in place with other souls, who will play an important part in its future incarnated life. And it is now time to 'join' the baby. This 'melding' of the soul with the child apparently happens six to ten weeks after conception, though it can happen all the way until the last moment, when the mother is giving birth. The subject explains:

> *"What is uppermost in my mind... the opportunity to live in the twentieth century. It's an exciting time of many changes. [...] I've met with the rest of the participants in my project [at the Recognition Class]. The signals... my compacts with people... yes, that's all done. I'm just gathering myself for... the big jump into a new life... there is apprehension... but I am excited too... [...] I say goodbye to everyone. This can be... difficult. Anyway, they all wish me well and I move away from them... drifting alone. There is no great rush... Pomar [my spirit guide] allows me to collect my thoughts. When I am quite ready he comes to escort me... to offer encouragement... reassurance... [...] We begin to move... at a greater speed. Then I am aware of Pomar... detaching from me... and I am alone... slanting away... through pillows of whiteness... moving away... passing through... folds of silky cloth... everything is blurred... I'm sliding down a dark tube... a hollow feeling... darkness... then... warmth! [...] I'm aware of being inside my mother. I'm in a baby – I'm a baby."*

> *"I'm busy with this new mind, even though it's not fully ready. [...] Once I attach to a child it is necessary to bring my mind into synchronization with the brain. We have to get used to each other as partners. [...] I am in the mind of the child but separate, too. [...] It's delicate and can't be hurried. [...] It's like a melding. There is an... emptiness before my arrival which I fill to make the baby whole. [I expand the intellect] that is there. We bring a comprehension of things... a recognition of the truth of what the brain sees."*

"I watch the parents. They might be having squabbles around the baby which sets up disturbing vibrations. I quiet the child as best I can. Reach out to the parents through the baby to calm them. I make the baby laugh in front of them by poking my parents' faces with both hands. This sort of thing further endears babies to parents. [...] I'm a bit anxious for my father... (giggles) He thinks he wants a boy, but I'll change his mind in a hurry!"

I wonder whether men—and women—would appreciate women's bodies more if they realized they are a gateway for bringing souls into physical reality. And would people appreciate their children more if they knew these little souls had *chosen* them? Seen in this light, the birthing process is truly a miracle!

> "I am told the most outstanding characteristic of the spirit world is a continuous feeling of a powerful mental force directing everything in uncanny harmony. People say this is a place of pure thought."
>
> Michael Newton, *"Journey of Souls"*

Journey of Souls: Case Studies of Life Between Lives by Michael Newton © 2002 Llewellyn Worldwide, Ltd. 2143 Wooddale Drive, Woodbury, MN 55125. All rights reserved, used by permission.

Conclusion – What Happens After We Die

Based on the revelations from Michael Newton's past life regression subjects, and out of-body and near-death experience subjects, the following sequence of 'events' would appear to be the norm in the spirit world after one's death:

1. Your soul is ejected from your body through your crown chakra. Occasionally, the soul might wish to remain around its loved ones for a little while, to console them.

2. A tunnel of light opens up, and the soul is pulled towards a bright, white light.

3. Your *"soul family"* and/or your spirit guide welcome you back. The feeling is one of relief, there is no pain, and one experiences an overwhelming sense of: *"Oh, wonderful, I'm home in this beautiful place again."*

4. Later, your essence is bathed by a bright beam of light, or a *'stream of liquid energy'*, in what is described sometimes as 'The Shower Of Healing'. Its purpose is to wash out any lingering negativity, allow you to let go of the bonds of your last life, and help you become whole again.

5. You then meet with your spirit guide to review your life. This initial orientation session with your guide prepares you to go before a panel of three to seven 'Elders'.

6. You have a meeting with your 'Council of Elders', who also review your life with you. The feedback you receive is based upon the original intent of your choices as much as the actions you undertook during your life. You get to express your frustrations and desires. They evaluate your perceptions of the life you have just lived and how you could have done better with your talents. They enquire as to what you did that was beneficial to others: *"How have you become more capable of loving? What lessons have you learned in this lifetime?"*

7. As you move through another tunnel, you finally arrive at your spiritual home where your 'oversoul' family resides. This is your spiritual family of fifteen or so souls. Members of the same

cluster group are closely united for all eternity. This is called the 'Inner Circle'. You are also part of a secondary, wider cluster of souls.

8. You then go to 'class' with the other members of your oversoul family. This involves looking through 'life books', picture books where you can see your past lives and alternatives you could have chosen. You are also shown glimpses of future possibilities, in the form of lessons.

9. Souls are also expected to spend time helping those on Earth (or other physical worlds) whom they have known and cared about. They go to a space some call *'The Place of Protection'*, where they mentally project outward their intention, *"holding and releasing positive vibrational energy to create a territory,"* in an attempt to comfort or effect change. Your spirit guides or guardian angels are watching out for you, and might send you some 'hints' or encouragement (see Chapter 4 where I describe examples of this in my own life).

10. When it is time to incarnate again into physical reality, you are taken to *'The Place of Life Selection'*. Once there, you get to use *'The Ring of Destiny'* which allows souls to preview different bodies, places, times, and circumstances for you to choose your new life from. The Ring sets up different experiments to choose from, and issues and situations for you to resolve on Earth, to gauge your abilities against the difficulty of these events.

11. Your soul consults with its spirit guide and peers about the physical and psychological ramifications of the new life and body choice you have made, and a final decision is arrived to.

12. Later you will be required to attend 'Recognition Class', with the ten to fifteen souls that are going to be close to you in your future life. Signals and clues are set up to be triggered at the appropriate time, for you to recognize them and those critical junctures in life.

13. Before leaving the spirit world, you meet with your Council of Elders again, for them to assess your motivations and the strength of your resolve towards working in this new body. They also remind you to honour your contract, demonstrate

persistence, and hold on to your values under adversity. They give you inspiration, hope and encouragement.

14. When you are ready, your spirit guide comes to escort you, and give encouragement and reassurance. You move through another tunnel, until finally you are inside your mother's womb. According to some accounts, this can happen at five months after inception, sometimes sooner, and occasionally it even happens at the last moment prior to birth.

This entire process from death to rebirth can happen relatively quickly – a few years or a few decades – or more than 1000 years might pass by until the appropriate circumstances are lined up for your next incarnation. Time is of little consequence in the spirit world.

Ultimately, the main lesson to draw from all this is...

There is divine perfection in all our lives...
You never really die... So you might as well live life to the full,
be happy, follow you heart and make a difference!

CHAPTER 3

What is The Meaning of Life?

What *is* the meaning of life then? Why are we here? What are we meant to *do* with our lives?

The answers to these questions provided below come directly from divine, spiritual sources, untainted by 'religious dogma'. Some flow directly from the unconscious of subjects under hypnosis—subjects from all walks of life, I should point out, with no spiritual leanings or knowledge necessarily, who don't even know or remember what they said while under hypnosis.

In other words, the people behind these quotes, below, have no agenda other than to share the truth about our spiritual origins. Ultimately it is down to you to use your intuition and *feel* whether this information resonates with you as being the Truth.

According to the channelled information in Neale Donald Walsch's book *Conversations With God*, 'God' explains our purpose as follows:

> "My purpose in creating you, My spiritual offspring, was for Me to know Myself as God. I have no way to do that save through you. [...] It was not enough for Spirit to simply know Itself as God... Knowing something, and experiencing it, are two different things. Spirit longed to know Itself experientially. [...] You can know

yourself to be generous, but unless you do something which displays generosity, you have nothing but a concept. You cannot experience yourself as what you are until you've encountered what you are not. This is the purpose of the theory of relativity, and all physical life. It is by that which you are not that you yourself are defined. Of course, there is no way for you to not be who and what you are – you simply are that (pure, creative, spirit), have been always, and always will be. So, you did the next best thing. You caused yourself to forget Who You Really Are. Upon entering the physical universe, you relinquished your remembrance of yourself. This allows you to choose to be Who You Are, rather than simply wake up in the castle, so to speak. You are, have always been, and will always be, a divine part of the divine whole, a member of the body. [...] <u>The deepest secret is that life is not a process of discovery, but a process of creation.</u>"

According to the passage above, the meaning of life is to discover and express *who and what you really are,* and thus create your life. By doing so you are expressing a new, unique facet of Source (God-Mind), allowing It to know Itself.

So, what do you want to CREATE next? Who do you want to be? Where do you want to live? What legacy do you want to leave behind? It is in your power to create whatever new reality you wish to experience.

Stewart Swerdlow seems to confirm what is mentioned in *Conversations With God* in his 'True Blood, Blue Blood' lecture. He states:

"God Mind does not know where it comes from. God Mind became conscious of itself. It was Lonely. It started to conceptualize, use its imagination... [...] <u>Your purpose: to discover who and what you are</u>. You are adding to the God Mind figuring out who and what it is."

> "<u>We are divine beings put here to evolve</u>, we have a divine purpose for being here. We're not just here to drive cars and go to work... <u>we're here to discover our true nature</u>. More and more of us are going to wake up to the fact that we are angelic beings... we're not just human... More and more people are going to have these psychic experiences. More and more people are waking up from the 'Matrix'."
>
> Jamie Passmore, intuitive

In yet another passage from *Conversations With God*, 'God' states that our souls are chiefly concerned with growing and evolving towards a higher spiritual plane:

> *"The soul is very clear that its purpose is evolution. That is its sole purpose – and its soul purpose. It is not concerned with the achievements of the body or the development of the mind. These are all meaningless to the soul."*

Michael Newton adds: *"The essential purpose of reincarnation is self-improvement."* He believes that our souls are progressing towards higher and higher levels of spiritual awareness, and that this process of self-growth is the reason why we are in physical reality. When asked whether this sort of self-actualization of the soul identity is the purpose of life on this world, a subject of his replied, simply: *"On any world."*

Another subject of his, under hypnosis, explains the meaning of life as follows:

> *"In the beginning there is an outward migration of our soul energy from the source. Afterward, our lives are spent moving inward... toward cohesion and the uniting.... There is an explosive release... then a returning... yes, the source pulsates. The source is all around us as if we were ... inside a beating heart... the source is endless. As souls we will never die – we know that, somehow. As we coalesce, our increasing wisdom makes the source stronger.*
>
> *Source desires to perform this exercise to give life to us so we can arrive at a state of perfection. To help the creator create. In this way, by self-transformation and rising to higher plateaus of fulfilment, we add to the building blocks of life. We came to Earth to be magnified... in the beautiful variety of creation. The source creates for fulfilment of itself. We think <u>what the creator desires is to express itself through us</u> by... birthing. I see the creator's perfection... maintained and enriched... by sharing the possibility of perfection with us and this is the ultimate extension of itself. We have to have faith in this decision and trust the process of returning to the origin of life. One has to be starving to appreciate food, to be cold to understand the blessings of warmth, and to be children to see the value of the parent. The transformation gives us purpose."*

Modern-day philosopher Dr. John Demartini, who has studied more than 30,000 books and texts, writes:

> "*We're here to learn, teach, and become our true nature, love and light*... *Inside every single person is an overwhelming desire to fully express their divinity, the absolutely spirit of love that they have and are.*"

Anita Moorjani states in her book *Dying To Be Me*:

> "*I understood that I owed it to myself, to everyone I met, and to life itself to always be an expression of my own unique essence. Trying to be anything or anyone else didn't make me better—it just deprived me of my true self! It kept others from experiencing me for who I am, and it deprived me of interacting authentically with them. Being inauthentic also deprives the universe of who I came here to be and what I came here to express. [...] I danced and drank champagne gleefully. I knew more than ever that life was to be lived with joy and abandon. I knew that the purpose of my life was to expand my tapestry and allow more and greater experiences into my life.*"

So how should you live your life, based on this information?

It's simple. Be loving. Be grateful for this gift called 'life'. Do what you do with love in your heart. Engage with life. Live with integrity. Experience joy. Connect with nature. Have fun. Discover your life purpose *and truly live it!*

> *How can you ever feel depressed when you know we are a part of God, we are all one, we are never alone, separation is an illusion, and we are loved and cherished forever?*

ALWAYS REMEMBER

You are loved and cherished, forever.

You have nothing to fear.

There is nothing you can do wrong.

PART II

The Stories

CHAPTER 4

When The Invisible World Meets The Visible World

Have you ever felt the realm of the Divine gently touch into your world? Perhaps you noticed a coincidence you couldn't possibly explain. You thought of someone and a moment later they called on the phone. Someone made a bizarre prediction about the future and it came true. Or perhaps you know of someone who had a profoundly life-changing, spiritual experience.

These are clues to the spiritual nature of our existence.

Some people find it hard to believe that they have someone looking after them 'from above'. After all, life can seem quite lonely and cruel at times. And yet our spirit guides provide us with insights or encouragement that can help illuminate the path we are meant to walk, at critical junctures in our lives, especially in periods of danger or great stress.

The following stories from my own life help illustrate why I believe beyond a shadow of a doubt that there is more to our world than meets the eye. *The spirit world is indeed very real!*

As you read the following account, I invite you, the reader, to think back to moments in your own life when the 'Invisible World' made 'contact'.

* * * * * * * * * *

"Tell The Driver To Shut Up And Look At The Road!"

Our taxi driver didn't even have time to hit the brakes. The 400-pound wild boar appeared seemingly out of nowhere, and we hit it at full speed, just a mile from our house. We were thrown about the vehicle like rag dolls. The car was totalled. And the poor animal lay dying in the middle of the road, blood spurting from its snout. Mercifully, it was all over in a matter of seconds.

Thirty minutes earlier I'd experienced something very unusual. My wife and I had flown home from our holiday in the Maldives, and during the taxi ride back to our house the driver kept looking at Mira in his rear-view mirror, while speaking to her in a loud and animated way. He was barely paying attention to the road. I didn't understand what he was saying, but he seemed to be an angry and high-strung man.

Suddenly, a voice in my head – or rather a fully-formed thought that did not originate from my own mind – said: *'Tell him to shut the f*** up and look ahead at the bloody road!'*. It would appear that my spirit guide doesn't shy away from using four-letter words to make his point…

Since I didn't speak the driver's language and my wife was engaged in conversation with him, I held my tongue. But I felt uneasy. A few minutes later, the thought *'OK then… brace yourself…'* entered my mind, as I was mentally shown a picture of someone raising their knees towards the driver's seat and placing their head between their arms, similar to the 'brace' position shown in airplane safety instructions.

Once again I ignored this advice, thinking it was just my imagination. Besides, we were about to reach our destination, and I didn't want to have a conversation with my wife along the lines of *"Honey, why are you curled up in a ball on the back seat of our taxi?"*, let alone have to ask her to join in, 'on a hunch'. A few minutes later, the driver crashed into that poor animal.

I walked the last mile to our house, shaken by the whole experience, and feeling sad for the boar. And then another thought crossed my mind.

"I don't know who that was, but… next time, I'll listen to my intuition!"

* * * * * * * * *

Chapter 4: When The Invisible World Meets The Visible World

Time is an illusion

People who have had a near-death experience or who have undergone a past-life regression, repeatedly state that 'Time is an illusion'. Everything is happening in the eternal moment of 'now'.

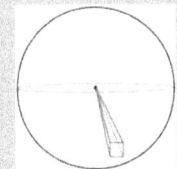

Imagine the Universe as being a hollow sphere, and our physical reality is a film being projected on the surface of the sphere. Time would be the illusion someone would experience as they travel in a linear fashion along the surface of the sphere, from one point on the surface to another. But to an observer at the center of the sphere, they would be able to see point A and point B at the same time. Perhaps it is from that central vantage point that our spirit guides can 'see' what is coming down the pike and help us correct our course.

* * * * * * * * * *

"Go To The Borders Bookshop in Town..."

As I look back on my life, I can see how in my moments of despair I was guided to take certain important actions. These were turning points, in my life.

In 2001 I was working as a security guard in Oxford, England. I had been suffering from depression for a number of years. One particularly miserable morning, I woke up with the thought *"Go to the Borders bookshop in town and buy books about 'Happiness'! You will begin your study on 'Happiness'!*

I walked into the bookshop later that day, and was directed to the self-help section. Not finding any books specifically about 'Happiness', I turned around and started heading towards the exit when I tripped over a small but hefty book titled *"GIANT STEPS"*. The toothy grin of author Anthony Robbins greeted me as I looked down. I had literally tripped over Giant Steps! *"How ironic,"* I thought to myself. And what was that book even *doing* there, in the first place? I'm certain it wasn't on the floor when I walked in!

Despite the book costing £6.99 – the equivalent of *more than two hours of pay* at my minimum wage job (£3.25 an hour) – I decided to buy it. *"If I only get ONE good idea from this book that helps my life in some way, it will have been worth the investment!"*

The book contained 365 tips and ideas for improving one's life, including an idea that made a lot of sense to me: *'modelling success'*. Other people have achieved what *you* want to achieve, so why not model the steps they took? If I wanted to find happiness, I decided, I would model people who are happy. *How do they think? What do they say? What actions do they take? What are their habits? What do they do with their time?* This exercise would eventually change my life and help me lift myself out of my depression.

This would not be the only time I would be 'guided' to buying a specific book. In 2004 I was in a bookshop in Stansted Airport, in London, on my way to a holiday by the beautiful Austrian lake of Klagenfurt. I was perusing the books on the lower shelves, looking for something to read on the flight, when my left hand shot up and landed on one of the top shelves. My gaze was still fixated on the lower shelf. When I looked up and to the left, I was holding the book *"The Celestine Prophecy"* (a book about recognizing the spiritual nature of our reality). A surreal experience.

Over the years, on a number of occasions three random people would recommend *the same book* to me within a few days of each other. I know to follow the signs now, and I order that book on the spot. Obviously 'someone' intends for me to read it!

* * * * * * * * * *

"What Have You Given?"

In 2003 I was fired from my job. After working as a security guard for a couple of years, I had been doing telesales for a training company on the outskirts of London, and I was earning only marginally more. I hated that job, and it showed in my attitude and my performance. After a rotten run of fourteen months where I only managed a single sale, I was unceremoniously (and unsurprisingly) let go.

I was a couple of months behind on my rent, and now I had no income. I tried looking for a job but none materialized. I was eventually thrown out of my apartment. Within three months of losing my job I found myself living in an abandoned building in London. A girl I had met told me that she and her bohemian musician boyfriend lived there, because *"Why pay rent, man, when there you can occupy a building for free?"*. The idea of squatting a building illegally sounded edgy and 'cool' at first, but the shine wore off pretty quick. For starters, me and these twenty or so homeless people didn't have electricity. I joined a local gym for £24 a month, so that I could have a hot shower and a shave from time to time. My eight (!) credit cards were maxed out. Luckily, this was the go-go years of the early 2000s, where banks would give credit to anything with a pulse. There were instances of people receiving credit cards in the mail made out to their *dog's* name... Whenever one of my cards would reach its limit and I couldn't pay the minimum deposit, the bank would magically increase the limit.

I lived like this for months. I was too embarrassed to admit to my friends or family back home in Greece what had happened. I kept thinking to myself *"You're pathetic... look at yourself... you should kill yourself and end it all..."*.

One particularly desolate day, I found myself laying in the mud in the Old Brompton Road cemetery, in London, crying in despair. I had run in there because I wanted to be alone, away from everyone. I was broke, unemployed, in debt, soaking wet and cold from the rain; I was ready to give up. They could just bury me where they found me. It *was* a cemetery, after all.

And then a thought entered my mind. A softly spoken voice, gently whispering to me...

"What have you given?"

This made me angry! What do you MEAN 'what have I given?' I'm BROKE! I don't HAVE anything TO give! Once more, patiently and softly, this voice whispered to me...

"What... have... you... given...?"

I looked up and noticed one of the 17th-century tombstones next to me. *"John Smith, 1622-1646, baker, father of three..."*. This man had died in his early twenties. It made me think, what would they put on *my* tombstone if my life ended that very day? And that's when I got angry a *second* time. There was nothing they *could* say! I hadn't *done* anything with my life! I hadn't *given* anything! *"Mark Anastasi... former security guard... dead!"* That's it!

I stood up, and vowed that this would *not* be the end. This was only the beginning. I made a vow: *"Come what may, I am going to turn this situation around, and then I'll devote my life to helping others do the same!"*

I walked out of that cemetery feeling the freest and happiest I had ever felt. I *knew* everything was about to change. Six weeks later I launched a digital publishing business and seminar company that would go on to become very successful, serving 40,000 customers worldwide.

It turns out, I still had a lot to give.

* * * * * * * * * *

> **Our Guides Give Us 'Hints'**
>
> "When we choose a body and make a plan before coming back to Earth, there is an agreement with our advisors. We agree... not to remember... other lives. Learning from a blank slate is better than knowing in advance what could happen to you because of what you did before. If people knew all about their past, many might pay too much attention to it rather than trying out new approaches to the same problem. The new life must be... taken seriously. Without having old memories, there is less preoccupation for... trying to ... avenge the past... [Our guides don't give us all the answers we need while on Earth] for the same reason we go to Earth without knowing everything in advance. Our soul power grows with what we discover.
>
> It's not a total blackout. We get flashes from dreams... during times of crisis... people have an inner knowing of what direction to take when it is necessary. And sometimes your friends can fudge a little... they give you hints, by flashing ideas."
>
> Michael Newton, *Journey of Souls*

* * * * * * * * * *

"Let Go of Control... Have Faith... and TRUST That You Are Taken Care Of..."

In 2013 I found myself experiencing a severe identity crisis. I wanted to take my business and my career in a different direction. I wanted to share more *profound* information with my clients and seminar attendees. But would it work? The company I had set up in London in 2004 had served tens of thousands of clients and had generated millions of dollars in the process. But this was different. Would people be interested in my new message?

I agonized over making this step. This change of direction could mean losing everything I had worked so hard at building. I was known for "marketing" and "wealth creation" seminars. What if no one was interested in my new books and the new message I wanted to share?

One night as I was trying to fall asleep, questioning who I wanted to become and worrying intensely about the future—going in circles in my mind about what I should do—a strong feeling of reassurance washed over me. It was a profound yet fleeting out-of-body experience. I have never experienced anything like it before nor since. An overwhelming, deep, soothing feeling of love, warmth, and reassurance flooded my body for a few instants as I received the message…

> *"… it is OK to let go of control… Relax, have FAITH, and TRUST that you are taken care of… You always have been…".*

I realized that for a very long time I had been trying hard to "control" everything in my life. Fighting, pushing, trying, stressing, to continue making money… out of fear: the fear of things going back to the way they had been before, when I struggled financially—or when my father had struggled financially. But now I could let go of that fear, and truly live my life according to my *real* values. In a sense, the book you are holding in your hands represents this new direction; a more 'profound' message I want to share with the world.

That night I slept the best I had in years.

* * * * * * * * * *

"You Need To Create The Space In Your Life For Your Children To Come…"

Sometimes the messages your spirit guides have for you come more clearly through people who are particularly 'tuned in'. My wife and I had been trying for a child for a number of years. At a seminar in London in 2013, one of the attendees – a very intuitive Austrian woman by the name of Ana Maria – told me:

"I have a message for you... The souls of your children are around you... You haven't gotten pregnant yet... because there is no 'space' in your life for your babies to come into... you are too busy!"

I was open to hearing what Ana had to say. Besides, she was right. I had been on 82 flights that year, visiting 17 countries to promote my book *'The Laptop Millionaire'* – and 300 flights in the previous five years alone.

It goes without saying that *stress* is one of the worst things you can have in your life if you want to be healthy or if you want to conceive a baby. Stress instantly puts you in a 'fight-or-flight' mode. It shuts down your digestion and elimination processes, for starters. It shuts down your body, to preserve energy. It's hard enough to get pregnant nowadays, without stress compounding the problem.

But Ana Maria was referring to something else. She said that the *souls* of our future children were *'around us'*, but they felt it wasn't the right time for them to *come* to us. They felt there was no 'space' for them in our life.

I took that message to heart. After all, it didn't hurt to try a new approach. Over the following weeks I changed my lifestyle. I cut back on my travelling. I ran fewer seminars. My wife took similar actions, training someone to run her workshops for her, to free up her time. I only worked from 9am to 2pm every day. The rest of the day was free for spending time with my wife, reading and learning new things, going for walks into nature with my Golden Retriever, playing basketball, swimming in the sea, etc. I wanted to communicate the message to the Universe, *"See? I'm creating 'space' in my life for our children! I'm ready!"*

I was proud of myself. This was some serious *intent* that I was demonstra-ting. But it would seem my spirit guides have a sense of humour... Just
two days after I changed my daily routine, the doorbell rang. I opened the door and found two children outside. They were our neighbours' kids, Ivanka and Jakub, 7 and 9 years old. They asked:

"Can we play basketball with you?"

They had seen me playing in my yard during the daytime – one of the perks of working from home. I answered: *"Oh, I'm sorry, I'm too bu...."* I was about to say 'busy', and then I caught myself. I looked up, and thought: *"You must be kidding me..."*. Surely the Universe was testing my resolve!

"You made a commitment, buster... now let's see you live up to it!"

I had a chuckle, turned off my laptop, and went outside to play with the kids. They didn't get to play with their father much because he was always busy with work. His (now ex-)wife would later tell us that he is a great provider for the family, but *"all the children want, is to spend time with their dad..."*. This is advice I've taken to heart since becoming a father.

Every afternoon, at around 4pm, these two children would ring my doorbell, and we would play football or basketball, go rollerblading around the neighbourhood, or play with my dog Leo. I've never heard of this sort of thing happening to anyone else. Do *your* neighbours' kids ring your doorbell and ask to play with *you*?

Creating that space—the fertile ground to invite the souls of our children in—was the first step we took. It wasn't the end of our journey, but we got pregnant eighteen months later... with twins!

* * * * * * * * * *

CHAPTER 5

Past Lives

In 2007, my wife Mira went to see a hypnotherapist in London, for a past-life regression. She did this out of curiosity, more than anything else.

The session began with the therapist putting her into a hypnotic state, and regressing her to when she was in her mother's womb. She then proceeded to ask questions about Mira's past lives. My wife relates the following account of that session:

> "She guided me mentally to a room down some stairs, and said: *'There will be doors in front of you... when you open this door... you will see a path to a past life... connected to an issue that you need to resolve...'*
>
> I saw lots of doors and got excited! I wanted to open the door in front of me. But suddenly, a power... whoosh... took me to a completely different door. The door opened – a very heavy door – but as I walked in it was pitch black.
>
> The therapist started asking *'Can you describe where you are? What can you see?'* I couldn't see anything. She then asked: *'Are you blind? Do you have a physical body...?'* It was pitch black, but I was not blind. *'In your mind, light a candle, to see around you...'* the hypnotherapist continued.

I realized I was locked in what looked like a cellar, or a well. It was circular. There was a really heavy door, and just a wooden stool. *'Do you know where you are?'* the hypnotherapist asked.

Suddenly, pictures started coming to me. I was locked underneath a chapel. I was really cold. I was sobbing. I could feel cold tears running down my face (the therapist put a blanket over me, at that point). I didn't have anything to eat... maybe pieces of old bread, that good people brought to me through a tiny opening in the wall...

As I was sobbing, she asked *'What are you doing there?'*, but I didn't know. *'Let's go back a few years... what's your name?'*, she continued. *'Jean'* came my response. *'I'm male'*, I said, (though it felt pointless to discuss my sex, as it is irrelevant in the spiritual realm). *'The year is 1640. I used to come to this chapel a lot, carrying big heavy books, going up these circular stairs. I used to go there quite a lot. I died there in 1643.'*

Then, in my mind, I went back to 1623. I was a young man, laying on the grass with my wife. I was in my twenties. I saw her with her back to me, linen white dress, long black hair. I was thinking how beautiful she is and how much love there is between us. I was so happy and content. I heard two children, laughing. Three or so years old, playing and jumping in the field. She turned around to me. I remember her big black eyes. She smiled at me with so much love.

My parents came to England from France and my name was Jean Bellevue. We lived on the border with Scotland, close to the sea on the East coast of England. In my house, there is a big table by the window, where I'm binding books. There is just one room in the house. We were poor. These books are in Latin. I can read them. I preach about freedom to the local people...

I was taken to another scene, years later. Suddenly, I heard lots of horses, lots of chaos outside. I heard my wife and children screaming. Soldiers. They are dragging my wife and children away. They are dragging me in a different direction. My house and other houses nearby are burning. I got locked up under that chapel…

'Who are these men?', the therapist asked. '*Arthur*', I replied. *'King Arthur?'* she continued. 'No, *Governor* Arthur'.

I felt so much sorrow. And guilt. It all happened because of what I believed in. I didn't know where my wife and children were… I was sobbing… and then suddenly I felt like something lifted me up out through the top of my head and out of my body. Like someone had released me, like a bubble. I was floating, with so much *light*. No more heaviness. I was out of my body. I saw myself below. I realized I had died. And suddenly… in a split second, everything made sense. I knew. I understood.

'Of course! It all makes sense now!'

This ball of light was taking me higher and higher… I was above the whole chapel… the village… my house… on the edge of the forest… feeling content and excited that *I'm finally going home*. Like I'd been away from home a long time. The spirit world was my home. *'Of course this is where I belong!'*

I was heading back to that place where everyone loves you, where there is no pain, where everything makes sense… I'd left all the pain *'down there'*.

I was aware of this strong light above me, pure LOVE… so much love, so strong, so powerful, like words can't describe. It was pulling me towards it. I was so happy to go there. It was the feeling of coming home.

Suddenly, as I looked below, I knew that my wife and my children were being held by the edge of the forest. I wanted to go to them. With the power of my mind I started moving towards them.

The light reassured me and soothed me, *'It's OK... let go...'*, pulling me towards it. You don't hear the words. It's just an instant knowing, an instant transmission of thought..."

* * * * * * * * * *

The surprising epilogue to this story is that there indeed *was* a Governor Arthur (the Governor of Newcastle), who worked for King Charles I, around 1640. At that time, they were locking up and killing everyone who stood against the King. Stories like this one are particularly meaningful to me, for they prove that *we have indeed experienced past lives!* We have existed in the spirit world. Death is not the end, but merely a return 'home'. We reincarnate. This implies the existence of a spirit world. By extension, does it not prove the existence of *God?*

* * * * * * * * * *

Chapter 5: Past Lives

"He Was Your Father In 1626..."

A couple of years ago a psychic named Leon, unaware of my background or my history with my father, revealed to me the following:

In **1452** my father and I were Greek, living in Constantinople (present-day Istanbul). He was my uncle in that lifetime. I was a young nephew of his, 10 years his junior.

We were taken prisoners in 1453, when Constantinople was invaded by the Turks. They gave us the choice to *"convert to Islam or die"*. I converted, and, being quite pragmatic, I was able to develop a good career under the Turks.

In 1461 the Turks expanded, and I ended up having to confront my then uncle. He was so upset with me that he tried to kill me, and in fact managed to wound me. My uncle was then captured by the Turks, and he was painfully killed by being cut into pieces. I was made to watch the cruel execution.

My mother in this lifetime was my aunt then – his wife. My uncle and her had looked after me when I was a boy. She was upset that I had repaid their love and affection by having her husband killed...

Leon proceeded to reveal to me another lifetime I shared with the soul of my present-day father.

In **1626** Greece was occupied by the Turks. My father resented the Turkish occupation, and he kept having problems with them. Eventually, after many altercations and provocations, his possessions were taken by the Turks. He was sent to prison and beaten. He naturally sent out many bad thoughts towards the Turks...

I was his son in that lifetime. I was more pragmatic, and very skilful at dealing with the Turks. My father disowned me for not being 'anti-Turkish' enough. I tried to help my father financially, but he said he didn't want my 'dirty money' (earned by "collaborating with the invader Turks"). My father needed medical treatment. Though he didn't want my money, the doctors took my payment anyway.

Mira was my wife in that lifetime as well. She was from Bulgaria (a Slav

Christian) and my father didn't accept her nor our three children because of our different religion (we were Greek Orthodox).

My mother in that lifetime was quite subservient to my father. I was the only surviving child, and she had to see me and the grandchildren secretly, to avoid his wrath.

The Present Day

My father was born in the 1950s, in a small village in Cyprus. He was sent to a boarding school in England, where he was subjected to bullying and abuse. When Turkey invaded Cyprus in **July 1974**, his family lost their land and their house, and they became refugees. He later ran an English-language newspaper in Greece, where he lambasted the Turks on a weekly basis for having invaded his native Cyprus.

As a result of these traumatic events, and other reversals later in life, he used antidepressants for over thirty years. His mood would fluctuate wildly over the course of a day, and he would regularly make us feel bad for having fun or enjoying ourselves *"because he had to work so hard to pay for everything."* I grew up feeling guilty for his depression and sadness, and for not being able to help him as a child.

I overcame my own 8-year depression using personal development. I did a lot of self-analysis to identify my negative beliefs and the root causes of my negative, depression-causing mindset. I modelled happy and successful people. I focused on my purpose and my goals, instead of focusing on the sorrow I felt in the past. I also changed my diet, eating more natural, organic food. I 'detoxed' regularly. This somehow helped clear negative emotions as well, and helped raise my 'vibration' or 'frequency'.

My father, unfortunately, rejected my many attempts to help him. He can be very stubborn and rigid in his thinking. He doesn't believe in alternative medicine, personal development, or anything spiritual.

A few years ago he had a stroke and incurred large hospital bills he couldn't pay. He wanted me to help him financially, while at the same time rejecting what he considered to be my *"dirty money"* (earned from selling ebooks online and from organizing 'wealth' and marketing conferences). I have always been more 'pragmatic' with regards to earning money, while he maintained a more naïve idealism.

My relationship with my father has been a sore point in my life. I spent half a decade not speaking to him. But as I gained a more spiritual perspective on things, through the years, I realized how *perfect* my father was for me to learn the lessons I needed to learn in this lifetime. His issues forced me to seek answers in personal development books and seminars. I wouldn't be where I am today if I had been born to any other family or any other father. For that I am grateful.

I also believe I chose to be born to my parents in this lifetime to heal the rift between us caused in the '1626' lifetime. Is it any wonder I felt guilty for my father's depression, as a child, following his brutal execution during that lifetime in Constantinople?

Furthermore, it is interesting to see that my father has chosen to be 'victimized' by the Turks for three lifetimes in a row… If you send anger out, then you are likely to get someone being angry with you. What you give out comes back. It took visiting the Northern side of Cyprus (occupied by Turkey) and meeting its inhabitants in 2008, for me to realize they are just regular people who wanted no part in the war or the occupation—events that were orchestrated by the 'powers that be'.

I hope my father will find it in his heart to forgive them, in *this* lifetime—and heal the issues he needs to heal in his heart—or else the karmic consequences will continue for him, lifetime after lifetime.

* * * * * * * * * *

Note: What situations keep reoccurring in *your* life? What problems keep coming up? What are these situations or problems trying to tell you? What is the *lesson* for you there? What do you need to *heal* in this lifetime?

* * * * * * * * * *

"This Is What Happens When You Steal a Camel…"

The reality of reincarnation raises important issues of morality and 'karma'. You should not harm anyone, as you would only be setting yourself up for an unfortunate outcome in a future life, to redress that imbalance and to have you learn the relevant lesson. British hypnotherapist and past-life-regression expert Nicola Dexter tells the story of how a client of hers kept complaining of the huge car repair bills she constantly had to pay, and how her car was always breaking down. She even bought a brand new car, and it *also* kept breaking down.

Under hypnosis it was revealed that in a past life in North Africa she had been a man who had stolen another man's camels, thus depriving him of his mode of transportation. She had to experience the anguish she had caused in her previous lifetime. After realizing and coming to terms with what she had done, and apologizing to the man through prayer, her transportation problems ceased.

Do not steal, cheat, harm, or kill, you would only be doing it to yourself!

There Is Divine Perfection In All Our Lives

I am now aware of a number of my past lives, involving my wife, my parents, and certain friends of mine.

Of course, I also have experienced issues that come up again and again. There are lessons I need to learn and issues I need to heal in this lifetime… Perhaps I will talk about these in a future book. I am learning to let go of my negative beliefs and habits, through love and compassion. Meditating on a daily basis definitely helps.

Recently, an English friend of mine suffering from painful Endometriosis for many years was told by her doctor that she needed to have a hysterectomy, for the pain to cease. She would not be able to have children.

What is bizarre, is that she recently discovered through a psychic reading that in a past life she had been a surgeon in France, performing hysterectomies and abortions, many of which had gone wrong. Guess where she currently lives… Paris!

In yet another lifetime, she died whilst giving birth, in India, in the early 20th century.

She has also been the victim of a number of attempted sexual assaults in this lifetime. She discovered during her psychic reading that in a lifetime in Russia in the 13th century, she was the son of a landowner who forced young girls working on the estate to have sex with him.

While some might view her current plight (painful Endometriosis) as 'Divine punishment', I believe it is simply what her soul *chose* in order for her to heal her past and become 'whole' once again. Is it not loving and compassionate to teach your children the error of their ways? Is it not wise to have them appreciate the consequences of their actions? Is it not loving to help them evolve into better people? Better souls?

It would not serve us to be sheltered from such realizations, however painful they may be.

A 4-year-old boy I know suffers from Muscular Dystrophy (nutrients and oxygen reach his muscles with difficulty). According to Leon, in the 5th century AD he had been a woman in Turkey who had caused a man to become weak and disabled. In the 20th century in Germany he was involved with the Nazis' plans for eliminating disabled children.

In a lifetime in the Marshall Islands in the 19th century, he was apparently the mother of a disabled child (his mother in this current lifetime), towards whom he was unkind. This young boy and his mother—the roles now reversed—have an opportunity to heal the pain between them, in this lifetime.

Once again, I should point out that his physical ailment in this lifetime is not a 'punishment'. He has chosen this body and this condition, for reasons all of his own, and it is exactly what his soul needs at this point in time.

While our society tells us people are 'victims' of disease or other unfortunate situations, perhaps <u>we ought to recognize and be grateful for the divine perfection that exists in all our lives</u>.

CHAPTER 6

The Miracle Man

Mira introduced me to her friend Glyn in 2010. Glyn is the author of *Eight Steps To Heaven*, and the creator of the *"11:11 Divine Mindset"* program containing channelled spiritual advice for mankind. Although he is by far the most remarkable psychic I have come across, his abilities extend beyond mere clairvoyance, as you're about to discover. In fact, he is known in certain circles in London as *'The Miracle Man'*.

When Mira first met Glyn some twenty years ago, she was working in a café in London. He was one of the regulars, and he told her one day: *"You are not going to work here for much longer... In about three weeks your life will change dramatically... Your face will be on a magazine cover."* He went on to tell her *"You will have a weird haircut"*, which he described in detail.

Three weeks later she was spotted by a modelling agent and she was hired that same day at a modelling agency. She later worked on a campaign by a high-end salon which ran trend-setting hairstyle fashion shows, and she had to sport a particularly bizarre haircut, exactly as Glyn had described it!

He also predicted to her, *"You will go back to live in Slovakia for two years, and you'll get a modelling contract in Milan."* Again, a sequence of events unfolded that led to her living in Slovakia and being hired by a modelling agency in Milan.

When he gets in a meditative state, Glyn has the ability to 'tune in' to what our spirit guides are communicating to us. I have been lucky enough to spend time with him over the years, and we've travelled to a few countries together. In the process, I have chronicled many stories from his friends and clients about his incredible ability that simply defies conventional thinking or scientific explanation.

When asked about his ability, Glyn explains that he's simply a 'channel' for this information. He can tune in to the messages our spirit guides are trying to communicate.

The stories in this chapter are offered up as further proof of the metaphysical nature of our reality. For if psychic abilities do indeed exist (the ability to communicate with our spirit guides), does this not prove that the spirit world is real?

****

"I See Books Everywhere!"

I had my first reading with Glyn in May 2010. He told me *"I see books everywhere. This is where you will become most successful. I see 'America', 'America', 'America'. Massive dealings in America."* Two years later, one of the 'Big 8' New York publishing companies handed me a contract to publish my first book, which became a New York Times bestseller and a Wall Street Journal bestseller. This indeed opened up many exciting new opportunities for me and my business across the US.

Glyn also told me *"When your net worth reaches one hundred million, you will own a part share in a major hotel chain."*

Over and over again, Glyn's predictions in my life have come true. He told me that my mother would *"leave Canada in September"* of that year. I didn't mention this to her, and lo and behold, on the 28th of September I received an email from her saying *"I've had enough. I'm leaving Canada and coming back to Europe."*

****

"In September You Will Meet a Man…"

In a reading for my sister, who had been single for many years and unemployed for more than a year, he told her: *"Don't worry. You will soon have your own business and you will make a lot of money. And in September you will meet a man. He looks Italian or Middle-Eastern. He is well dressed. You will meet him in a country that is neither his nor your own, and you will travel with him all around the world."*

She stayed at our summer house in Cyprus for a few months, where I had her working on her mindset and doing some mental 'release work'. I also taught her some of my business strategies. Within three months she started her own business—a highly successful social media management company—and met her future husband at a seminar in London. He's Australian… but his parents are originally from the Middle East!

They were married less than a year later, and have travelled extensively all over the world since!

* * * * * * *

"There Will Only Be a Small Window of Opportunity To Get Your Funds Out…"

Glyn continued to astound us with his ability. His remarkable gift would come to our rescue in the most unexpected way.

In 2014, the Cypriot government —in the throes of a severe banking crisis— took the extraordinary step of taking over a foreign-owned local bank with billions in deposits. I would later find out they used the funds to prop up their local banking system. Customers—my company included—could no longer access their funds. I was forced to let go of my staff and shut down my business.

Although the bank assured its 5,000 or so international clients that the issue was only temporary, the weeks went by and still no one could access their accounts. Glyn told me: *"Don't believe what they are telling you on the phone. You need to fly there and meet the bank staff in person. This isn't going to be resolved any time soon. There will only be a small window of opportunity for you to get your funds out... so you need to take action, and fast."*

I decided to fly to Cyprus as soon as possible. Glyn advised me further: *"You will be greeted by someone at the reception desk. They will take you to the offices upstairs. You will enter a room, where there will be two desks – one with a man, the other with a woman. Speak to the woman. She will be able to help you."*

Sure enough, a few days later, upon arrival at the bank, I was brought into an office, where there were two staff – a man and a woman. I spoke to the woman. And the information I was told was *very* different to what had been said to me by their customer service department over the phone.

I found out that clients could fax a request to the bank for a withdrawal, up to €10,000 a day, Monday to Friday. The cheques would be issued within a couple of weeks. Most customers didn't take advantage of this, as they expected their accounts to be activated again soon. But I knew better.

Every day, diligently, over a period of a few months, I sent out a fax to the bank. Glyn told me I wasn't out of the woods yet, and that there would be a few hurdles to overcome still.

He was right. A few weeks later I flew back to Cyprus to collect the cheques, but was told that no bank in the world would cash them, apart from one of the local banks *"Why is that?"* I asked. *"Because they are the bank issuing the cheques"*, came the reply.

Glyn advised me every step of the way. Suffice to say that the local banks tried to make the whole process as arduous and asinine as possible. Thanks to Glyn, I was able to navigate through that bureaucratic maze and got the funds out just in time. Shortly thereafter, clients could only withdraw €1,000 a day, and then only €200 a day. Now, the bank has been shut down. Thousands of account holders will undoubtedly never see their funds again.

The window of opportunity that Glyn had mentioned was closed.

* * * * * * *

"He Clicked His Fingers And The Cyst Disappeared!"

Glyn's miracles in our lives would not end there. My wife and I had been struggling to conceive for many years, as I've mentioned previously. When a test showed a large cyst in one of her ovaries, she asked Glyn if there was anything he could do to help.

Glyn simply replied, *"It's done"* as he clicked his fingers. He then told her to go get checked again on a certain date. She did, and to the doctor's total astonishment the cyst had completely disappeared as though it was never even there. A miracle. Two months later we were pregnant!

"People around the world claim to have powers of healing, but I am witness to the real power of miracles of God working through a living man on the Earth", Mira would later write.

More recently, my assistant was also experiencing difficulties in conceiving a child. Doctors mentioned issues relating to 'uterine fibroids'. During a reading she had with Glyn, he said: *"I've clicked my fingers, it's done – you will now have a child. You have been given this child by God."*

A month later she was pregnant.

* * * * * * *

In 2014 Glyn was staying with us at our house in Athens. He joined us in the garden, one evening, with tears in his eyes. He was visibly emotional. He told us: *"You are going to become parents soon… the soul of your child just spoke to me, in the bathroom… I just had a conversation with your child… It told me 'I'm on my way… I'll be there soon…'".*

That evening he also told us: *"Your dog, Leo, already senses that you are not going to give him as much attention, when the children come, and he feels sad about this…".* Dogs are much more intuitive than we give them credit for. Experiments have shown that dogs know when their owner *intends* to come home, even if the owner is miles away. Our Golden Retriever knew that Mira was going to get pregnant before we did!

* * * * * * *

"Wimbledon Tennis Champion Pat Cash Miraculously Healed From Back Pain"

Glyn's abilities have grown significantly in the past year, and they continue to do so. He recently helped former Wimbledon tennis champion Pat Cash, who wrote the following acknowledgement:

"With severe back pain and a diagnosis of two herniated discs and two obliterated discs, it seemed that the thousands of hours of high-intensity tennis had finally taken their toll. I spent thousands of dollars on physical therapy and cortisone injections but it only ever provided temporary relief. The pain was terrible. Standing up straight was just about the most painful thing as the pressure went right on to the bulging disc that was pressing against the nerves.

I was discussing my problem with Glyn one day over the phone, as friends do, and he asked if he could try healing me. Glyn explained that he had some successes recently and that one of these successes was with a friend who had a large cyst on her ovary. He explained that with the help of spirit guides, he managed to make it disappear completely, simply by using his mind. A real life miracle.

I was more than happy to give it a try, as I was running out of any earthly possibilities. Glyn was told (by his higher source) that I wouldn't need surgery, that everything would be OK, and that I should trust. By using his mind he looked inside my back and described what he was seeing. He said it was like a 'white sticky kind of glue or cement' with black spots all around two joints in my lower back. According to the scans I had previously, there were two bulging discs but at either end of my back so I thought he was wrong.

As Glyn described it, he and his guides proceeded to put a 'golden ball of healing light' into the lower back area that he had seen. After 10 minutes over the phone, he told me that the golden light would continue to heal me, that it would be a few weeks before I started getting some relief, and that it would continue until I was healed. Glyn also gave me some rehabilitation advice, and gave me the 'all clear' for people I should work with for my back, as well as people I should avoid.

> *I went back to the doctors to have further check-ups, and lo and behold, the sticky cement Glyn had spoken of was diagnosed as being fibrous white scar tissue, which had formed after an injury. The expert also mentioned that I had the scar tissue around two discs in my lower back, which was causing misaligning of the joints. He also said the upper disc was not a problem. How could Glyn have known this?*
>
> *It's been almost 3 months since Glyn's healing and I'm 90% pain free. I'm playing tennis, doing yoga, putting my shoes on, getting in and out of the car and getting up and down off seats, all without pain. Sceptics can call it what they will, but what I do know is that some amazing things have happened recently and that healing has taken place. This could only be [described as] a miracle."*

A man is performing miracles in London, casually, like it's nothing, and he shuns the spotlight, the media, wealth and fame. Now *that* is a story worth talking about, wouldn't you agree?

* * * * * * *

"George Died Years Ago, In The War!"

Glyn first became aware that he might be a bit 'different' when he was 5 years old. One day the doorbell rang, and he went to open the door. A man wearing a soldier's uniform was standing there. It looked like a uniform from the First or Second World War. *"You're Glyn, right?"* the man enquired. *"Yeah!"* replied the little boy. *"Is your grandmother here? Can you please go and call her? Tell her that George from St. Mary's is here."*

Glyn ran up the stairs to get his grandmother. He relayed the message, to which she replied *"Yeah, right... George died years ago, in the war!"*

* * * * * * *

"Your Grandfather's Watch... It's Yours Now."

Mira's boyfriend at the time when she met Glyn didn't believe in any of this 'psychic nonsense'. Glyn said *"Bring him to me"*. During the reading he gave him, Glyn proceeded to tell him everything about his childhood, including his secret hiding places that nobody else knew about... Glyn then said, *"Your grandfather is showing me a Swiss watch, wrapped in a handkerchief. He says 'It's yours now'"*, showing the hand motion of the watch being presented to him.

Mira's boyfriend started crying. In his childhood, he would go to his grandfather's study and take out that watch, to look at it. A wealthy man had given it to his grandfather in exchange for his service.

Three months later his grandmother passed away. When he returned home, his mother handed the antique watch to him, wrapped in a handkerchief, with the exact same hand motion as Glyn had demonstrated. She said: *"Your grandfather wanted you to have this..."*

* * * * * * *

"Don't Ride Your Bike To Work!"

During a reading for a construction worker in London, Glyn said: *"Be very careful when riding your bike to work. Don't ride it to work the next two weeks. You'll have an accident and dislocate your shoulder."*

The client was spooked, but the next day on the building site he dismissed the whole thing, and made light of it.

Two weeks later a car drove into him and his entire arm had to be in plaster. He couldn't work, of course, which meant a significant loss in his earnings.

* * * * * * *

"Do You Really Want To Know?"

Another time, a Polish client of his asked whether his wife was cheating on him. Glyn refused to answer the question, saying it wouldn't be right for him to reveal such things. The client kept insisting, and goaded him for an answer. *"Come on! I've paid you money! Tell me the answer? What? You don't know?"*

Again, Glyn declined, but the client kept insisting, over and over again, asking for his 'money's worth'.

Finally, Glyn relented. He described the man's house in London, *to the last detail*. He described the staircase in the house. He said *"Do you really want to know…? I see you going down that staircase, leaving at 7am, and another man coming in from a different entrance."*

At the insistence of the client, he then proceeded to describe the man, and even mentioned the man's name, pronouncing it *in Polish* (Glyn doesn't speak Polish).

"I knew it!" the man exclaimed. *"It's my cousin! I even brought the son-of-a-b**** to England and got him a job!!"*

* * * * * * *

"Am I Really Seeing This?"

On one occasion, Mira was acting as an interpreter for an Eastern European man, a mutual acquaintance, who wanted a reading from Glyn. There was a moment of silence before Glyn began, as he got into a more meditative state. Mira closed her eyes.

Suddenly, she saw the spirit of a very old woman, holding a wooden stick, walk into the room. The spirit went up to the client sitting at the table… and placed her hand on the client's shoulder! Mira held her breath and thought to herself, *"If Glyn says something about this, it means that what I am seeing is real!!"*

A few moments later, Glyn opened his eyes, ready for the reading to begin. The first words out of his mouth were: *"There is an old lady standing next to you."*

* * * * * * *

"Yes, It Was Your Grandfather..."

On another occasion, Glyn turned to Mira and simply said, out of the blue, *"Yes, it was your grandfather. That is the answer to your question."*
Mira had gone to Windsor Castle on a sightseeing trip, and walked into the chapel that exists on the castle's grounds. She heard the beautiful singing of a children's choir, and closed her eyes to enjoy the moment. Suddenly she felt a reassuring, loving hand on her right shoulder. The message came: *"Don't worry, everything is going to be fine."* She had been meaning to ask Glyn whether that message had come from her grandfather...

Glyn added: *"Your grandfather is here. He's showing me something... flour... potatoes... eggs... salt... you put it together like dough, making pancakes on a stove... and now he's throwing them at you, saying 'Don't cry my little raisin!'..."*

That's what he used to call Mira. Her cousin Ivanka and her used to throw the pancakes at each other, and their grandfather would get upset at them for wasting food...

* * * * * * *

"Shall We Freak Them Out?"

Glyn's mother also happens to be a gifted psychic. When she was visiting Glyn a few years ago, she mentioned that she really wanted to meet Mira. When they finally met, Mira felt like they had been family in a past life. *"She was looking, staring at me! I was thinking, Oh my God, what does she see?!"* She didn't have to wait long for a reply.

> *"You have an amazing golden aura around you. It is very rare. It means you have powerful healing abilities. Many years from now, you will heal with your voice."*

Indeed, some fifteen years later Mira became a hypnotherapist. And yes, my wife does indeed possess a wonderful 'golden aura' about her. :)

They all went out for a picnic that day, in the garden of Glyn's apartment block in London. Two teenage girls were at one of the windows, overlooking the garden, and started sending little papers at them, giggling. Glyn turned to his mother and said playfully, *"Shall we freak them out? OK... what's her name?"*

After a few minutes, Glyn turned to the girls, and proceeded to tell them their names, the name of their dog, what their mom did for a living, and so on. The girls were flabbergasted. *"Oh my God, how do you **know** this?!!"*

* * * * * * *

"John Lennon Is Giving Me Some Tunes"

In his mid-twenties, Glyn started channelling music and lyrics. They would simply appear in his mind, fully-formed. *"I'm going to be a musician. I need to write music"*, he told his friends. He bought a second-hand guitar. Within a year he was writing music and playing half a dozen instruments. This ability seemed to just come out of nowhere.

Glyn was at a friend's house one day, attending a party. There was a piano there. He sat down and just started playing. Everyone was astonished at his virtuoso performance. *"Wow! Where did you learn to play the piano like that?!"* they exclaimed. His reply took them by surprise. *"I don't know. This is the first time I ever touch a piano. I just know I can do it. If you KNOW you can do something... then you can. John Lennon is giving me some tunes... I sometimes work with him..."*

* * * * * * *

"He Started Describing My Apartment, In Detail!"

Many of his clients are amazed at his ability to *see* them and their environment during a reading, while sitting halfway across the world.

I was aware that psychic 'remote viewing' was possible, but to most people it is an alien concept.

"I don't know how Glyn did this, but although he was halfway across the world from me, he started describing my apartment IN DETAIL, the view from my apartment, and even the books in the bookshelf behind me!" wrote one astonished client.

Another client said, *"I was continuously surprised at just how much Glyn knows about me. He knows about my job... how my office looks like inside-out and the people giving me a hard time... the colour of my car... my childhood struggles..."*

* * * * * * *

"Your Little Boy Is Trying To Get Your Attention"

"You had an abortion, didn't you?" The question took his client by surprise. She replied that she hadn't.

Glyn stayed quiet for a moment, and then said, *"Yes... you had an abortion..."* and proceeded to tell her at what age it happened, and under what circumstances. She broke down in tears, and admitted that it was true. She had never told anyone.

Glyn continued: *"Your little boy is here. He is 4 years old. You never got over it. You feel guilty about it. You cry over it at night... He wants to tell you that he's fine, he's around you and he is trying to cheer you up."*

Glyn then added: *"You always have issues with your tights, don't you?"* She was constantly buying new pairs of tights, and within five minutes they would get ripped. Her co-workers would often tease her about this.

"Your little boy is trying to get your attention and cheer you up, by pulling on your tights!" Glyn explained.

By realizing that her child was alright, and by coming to terms with what had happened, she was able to forgive herself and move on. She hasn't had any issues with her tights since that day, either.

* * * * * * *

"The Polyp Has Completely Gone"

Carmena from New Zealand is another testament to Glyn's extraordinary healing ability. She writes:

> *"I had gone to my doctor for a routine check-up and they found that a polyp was blocking my cervix. I was referred to a specialist to have it*

removed, but I wanted to avoid surgery, if possible. During our reading, Glyn described what he was seeing inside of me. He said that he could see the polyp and that he was using his mind to remove it. Just over a week later, I went into my doctor's. The polyp had completely gone. The doctors were amazed. The profound feeling of peace and well-being was tremendous. Even to this day I cannot possibly explain how Glyn was able to achieve this. There really is only one way of looking at this: It was a real miracle."

* * * * * * *

"I Am Sending Spirit Guides Into Your Womb To Heal The Problem"

Melissa Anne, from Miami, USA, had the following experience to share:

"I had a car accident in December 2014 while I was almost 28 weeks pregnant. I went straight to hospital, we were informed that the impact from the accident had caused "placenta previa" (the placenta was blocking the neck of the uterus), and there was bleeding in my uterus (the cervix split and blood was seeping in). They had to prepare me for an early C-section. I signed the documents and they prepped me for surgery. I was heartbroken and terrified. I contacted Glyn and asked him if there was anything he could do. I knew he was gifted from God and had powers that were not of this Earth…

He told me not to worry and that he was sending spirit guides into my womb to heal the problem and to watch over us. He said that he could see me sitting in a rocking chair with a cup of tea and a fat belly, so I knew then that we were going to be ok.

That evening I had another ultrasound. When I looked at the pictures of my ultrasound I couldn't believe my eyes. There were <u>faces</u> in the ultrasound picture. I thought I was going crazy. Glyn told me I wasn't crazy, and that he had told me they were coming already. He had sent them to watch over us.

> Two days later we got out of hospital on bed rest as the hematoma had miraculously healed itself. My daughter came into this world when she was supposed to. Now when I look at my happy little angel Amaya-Jane I couldn't be any more thankful. She really is a miracle baby and Glyn is an angel sent from above. Thank you simply isn't enough."

* * * * * * *

"I Want To See The Sun Shine Over The Sea…"

A friend of ours tragically lost her baby daughter a couple of years ago, a month after she was born. There had been complications at birth, and the baby was rushed to the Emergency Room. The doctors put her on a respirator, due to a problem with her lungs. We didn't mention that to Glyn, but simply sent him a message asking if he could help. He said he was told to *'breathe some air into her lungs',* and that he was communicating with the child's soul (how could he have known about her *lungs?*).

Despite a negative initial prognosis from the doctors, the little girl started getting better, and was even taken off the respirator after a while. Glyn's message to us:

> *"I feel the child already, her heart is very weak and her breathing is shallow. They need to wait and see, it's a 'tests' and waiting game right now. I have blown more air into her lungs and the eyes are becoming more aware of the surroundings. I was told to blow the child a kiss of life. How long that will be for is up to the child now."*

> *"It is amazing what the soul of the little one is telling me… she says: 'I will decide whether to stay or go – but I do want to see the sun shine over the sea…'."*

This sentence makes me cry every time I think of it. Souls often describe choosing to come back to Earth because of the flowers, the trees, the birds, and the natural beauty on our planet… In the evenings, as the sun sets on the southern part of Cyprus, the way it glimmers off the sea is a stunning sight. There is something that feels divine, uplifting, and peaceful in that moment. It nourishes the soul. No wonder the little girl's soul wanted to experience it…

Eventually, heartbreakingly, the soul of the child told Glyn it had to go.

"I cannot stay... I have to leave. This body would not allow me to do what I came here for..."

The doctors decided to operate on the child's lungs. Glyn wasn't told of this decision, and yet he 'saw' that something was happening with the child's blood. The baby died a few days later from an infection in its blood, due to the surgery. The child had chosen to go, reassuring its mother with the words *"Do not worry, I am well. I will come back."*

Two years later, our friend gave birth to a healthy little girl. :)

* * * * * * * * * *

What Does This All Mean?

What are the implications of Glyn's ability?

1. God exists. The spirit world confirms this to Glyn all the time.
2. We have spirit guides, guiding us from 'the other side'.
3. Reincarnation is real. We never really die.
4. We choose our body and our parents, prior to reincarnating.
5. We can affect the world around us with the power of our mind.

Of course, talk of miracles is anathema to "conventionally-minded" scientists. *"This is not possible!"* they'll exclaim. And yet...

* * * * * * * * * *

Glyn's Predictions

On the 31st of July 2015, Glyn made a series of predictions, which he sent to me via email. He predicted that a terrorist attack would occur in a crowded marketplace in the Philippines, in August 2016. One year later, a bomb exploded in the busy market of Davao City in the Philippines, killing twelve people and injuring 60. The government knew of this attack two days before (in August) but they chose to ignore the threat.

His second prediction simply read: *"Osaka Japan – October 2016 – Natural disaster."* A year later, in October 2016, a 6.2-magnitude earthquake hit the city of Osaka, affecting 80,000 households.

His next predictions are altogether more chilling...

"War Breaks out between Syria and the USA December 2018."

"Worldwide Health epidemic January 2022."

"The United States of America will completely and utterly collapse..."

My Interview With Glyn

Glyn is very low-key about his abilities. He rarely – if ever – speaks of them to people outside his inner circle of friends and private clients. Most people are too closed-minded and indoctrinated (whether by 'religious' dogma or 'scientific' dogma) to react with anything other than cynicism—or fear.

And yet the world is such dire straits today that he feels compelled to reach out to more people with his message. He recently granted me an interview, the first he has ever agreed to. I asked him about his abilities, his purpose, and how he feels about what is happening in the world today. His closing comment brought a stark warning for humanity...

I began the interview by asking him about the moment he realized he had an uncommon ability:

> *"The initial gift, what people would call clairvoyance, I suppose, began when I was 17. I literally started knowing things about my friends. And it just kept going on and on. I would know things about them and be able to see things, which would then happen. That's what confirmed to me that the gift was real. They would react with curiosity, excitement... sometimes shock. By the time I was 18 I was doing readings all over the UK, and various other places."*

> *"The beginning point for me was a sense of clairvoyance, being able to see, visions, different words... from the divine... And as I've grown, other abilities have come. Remote viewing, healing... I feel like there is a sense of 'doorways' that have opened up in me. I sensed a shift in awareness. An overall transitional state towards sublime awareness."*

One of my first questions to Glyn was simply *"How do you do it?"* His reply surprised me.

> *"I don't need to know how I do it exactly but I can give you a sense of what I do. With regards to looking into people's pasts for example, and identifying actual moments that need to be addressed for someone, I will see those actual moments that have happened, describing what has happened in detail. I do this by what feels like stopping time*

within my subconscious, while remote viewing so that I can stretch that moment in time, giving me the opportunity to visually look into the moment and read the feelings of the moment. Of course, this is only one point of understanding the way in which the gift truly works but most certainly helps to identify truth over fiction, as of course it is 'impossible' to be able to read the past of someone you have never met before, right? And yet that is precisely why so many people have come back to me time and time again, simply because I show them things that they know are without doubt turning the 'impossible' into the possible."

Mark and Glyn at the Anassa hotel, Akamas Peninsula, Cyprus

"When others will ask me, as they often do, 'how I do this', I reply "the answer is simple: it's a gift from God. I'm doing the work of God". It's not something from the normal conscious domain where people live. It doesn't exist in this world, it's from another dimension, so to speak, and it comes through somebody to give to others, if it is that person's purpose."

"Many refuse it. They don't want the responsibility. Some are given these abilities but they walk away from it, out of fear. Or maybe God decides that they are not ready and He allows them to walk away gently and then chooses another host."

> *"As you know I am not religious whatsoever. **God is within everybody.** God is available to everybody. But a few are chosen… to be given these abilities… for them to walk forwards and help others."*

> *"Because this is my purpose, because this is for God, it has enabled me to transition into using the power of my subconscious on a very, very high level. Scientists will never understand what happens in the subconscious minds of people like myself."*

Since he raised the topic, I asked Glyn about what he felt the purpose of his work was.

> *"<u>My purpose here involves changing people's lives for the better, opening their minds to awareness, to divinity</u>, helping them get rid of the issues that live in their conscious mind, helping them to get closer to the higher levels of divinity, (their own higher awareness) so that they are walking a divine path. And of course to heal people if necessary. <u>My purpose in a nutshell is to change the way people think and are evolving on this planet.</u>"*

> *"Scientists could continue to try and understand people like me for the rest of eternity and they never will. How can scientists explain remote viewing? Remote viewing is a complete mystery because how can anybody be in one place at a certain time, and see into another place in the world, and describe what is around them at that moment in time using nothing but their mind? The only way I can describe that possibility is that I am somehow using the divine part of my subconscious mind to 'time travel' with the help of my soul."*

I made an observation about how people seem to have lost a sense of meaning in their lives. They are desperate for *substance*, and they seem to have reached a 'bottom of emptiness'. Glyn agreed, and added:

> ***"Humanity is going in the wrong direction… because of fear in their conscious minds.*** *They have lost faith. Everybody is trying to always control everything. <u>The key to life is to let go and be present with life, to find the pathway to the inner God to find divinity</u>. They've walked away from God, because they don't believe that he lives within them, and because they have allowed the conscious mind to take over and rule them. <u>People didn't simply walk</u>*

away from God... People walked away from themselves. They're looking at God 'externally', like something to 'look up' to, outside of themselves."

"They've allowed the conscious mind to take over, rather than the subconscious where God lives. **It is the conscious mind that creates the fear, the anxiety, the selfishness, the anger, frustration.** *It's not a pure space. People have walked away from their true self... Humanity has walked away from the Divine within."*

"Love and compassion will give you a head start. The understanding that love is the source power that one needs to move forwards. Love is a catalyst to the greatness and the glory of the divine. What Jesus originally stated or wanted was peace on Earth, abundance of a loving nature, to be selfless, to be unconditional, to love thy neighbour, he wanted people to open their eyes, to be less judgmental, to naturally be giving, to love their fellow man and woman, he wanted everybody to walk forward into the space of love. <u>Love is the greatest key to the human existence</u>.*"*

"Humanity is going in the wrong direction because simply people have lost faith. They believe what people of the past have said... in texts... you can look at the way people believe what they see in the media... it's all a laughable, huge joke."

"Amongst the people I see selfishness, greed, anger, tyranny, war, chaos. Because they are walking away from love. Everyone is trying to control everything, control man, control the daughter, control money, etc. because they are fearful, and they don't understand that the key to love is to let go, be in the present and have faith in your heart and soul. Many people make all their decisions based on fear: fear of being alone, fear of not being good enough, fear of not paying the mortgage... <u>The only answer, the only way to conquer the fear is by walking with the Divine</u>, *and that is what my purpose is."*

When I enquired about how he was able to heal people at a distance, simply with the power of his mind, he replied:

"I've been able to somehow, because of this gift, understand how to bend matter, space, time... the only way I can describe it is my soul

was flown from me and went right down inside this woman's body... I could see the issue... I said don't worry about it, I will take it away. I said to her that I would send spiritual guides who walk with me, from the Divine space, into her womb to heal her. And that's what happened."

Glyn also explained, that he sees a golden light form in his mind, within the area of the body that needs healing, he says that once he sees this, and if God decides, that this is meant to be, the job will be done. He added: *"It is impossible to do this... unless it was a miracle from God himself."*

"I am just a vehicle, just a host, a channel. The words that are coming from me are channelled from the divine. Through my teachings I help people cleanse and create closure within the conscious mind. It enables them to rid away all their conscious fears, and have the subconscious mind take control of the conscious mind. I explain how to protect themselves from everything that is negative, that can affect their lives. I then teach people how to access divine psychic messages themselves."

"The greed of religion, the greed of the leaders, the greed of the minority, the greed of the majority... This world of greed obviously means people are governed by the darker forces. The selfish and the greedy people of this world are walking with the devil".

"If the people continue to walk in the direction they are going currently... this mindset of walking away from their true path, having lack of empathy for others, focusing on the material, focusing on climbing the career ladder at the expense of everything else... living the way of the greedy... without any divinity in their lives... the world will finish in the way we know... The people of the world will drive themselves into a pit of fury... <u>a huge expanse of flames and destruction and chaos. That is where the world is heading unless people correct their course.</u>"

"Without divinity on their side people will continue to walk selfishly in their own life, in their own space without a need and care for anyone else."

"So many people in this world are so corrupt, selfish, and greedy, that <u>if Jesus Christ were to reveal himself today, in our modern world, people would be fearful</u>, and most likely do as they did before and crucify him. They want it... but when it arrives they are afraid of it. Jesus coming back is just one example of what many people have wanted their entire lives, this is what they have waited for their entire lives, but when it arrives they will be fearful. It would be something outside of their control. So they judge, because they are threatened. That's why they are afraid when true miracles happen."

"The devil – the negative forces within the universe – wants everyone to control everything around them and not let go. The conscious mind always wants to hold people in a state of fear, always wants people to look forward, trying to grasp something, so the devil can keep them under its control. Oh, I want to make that money, I want to be a pop star, I want to make a million pounds... But what about true purpose? Maybe being wealthy, materially, is one's true purpose, but without reaching inside to find one's divinity, how would one know?"

"We are at a crucial moment in time. *A crossing. A point of no return. Choosing to walk with the divine... That's how we'll fight the spiritual war that is existing beneath what people can see. The divine mindset has to be pushed through to help change this, so that we can go back to what the Gods first wished for this place, Earth, to be. A place of all peace and love, strength and will and faith. We must find the God within whether our God is Christ, Allah, or Buddha and we must search to find the true source of wisdom that exists within."*

"You have to be a WARRIOR on this Earth to take on board what the divine show you. You have to be literally a warrior... because we are at war between good and evil. And because we are the minority at the moment."

* * * * * * * * *

I feel particularly privileged to know Glyn personally. While he has kept a low profile all these years, the time is right for more people to become aware of him. The world needs him.

The things I have seen Glyn do can only be described as *a miracle*, at a time when people have lost all faith. In our cynical world, he is a daily reminder that the Divine is all around us, and that *"walking with the divine"* is humanity's only way forward.

You can get in touch with Glyn at www.1111isHere.com (*Eleven Eleven Is Here*).

PART III

The Insights

CHAPTER 7

10 Spiritual Insights That Will Change Your Life

Developing a spiritual understanding of our world deeply transforms one's perspective on life and what it means to be alive. It also makes it considerably easier to feel happy, content, grateful, inspired, and loving towards others on a day-to-day basis. Isn't this better than the cynical and empty 'Philosophy of Futility' alternative?

This spiritual perspective on life states that we are spiritual beings experiencing physical reality in the body of a human. We are a part of the 'God-Mind'. We are here to *create* our lives and become fully self-expressed. Physical reality is not 'real', it is merely a 'stage' for us to express ourselves and *experience* things. We never really die. Our soul goes on forever. We are loved deeply and forever. Everything around us is 'energy', and this energy is malleable to human intention and thoughts. We create our lives... our outward reality... with our thoughts.

What are the implications regarding how we should live, day-to-day? In this chapter I share ten spiritual insights that have the power to change your life for the better.

Insight #1: You Are Never Alone

According to Michael Newton, each soul incarnated on Earth has a spirit guide with which the soul communicates. It offers comfort and guidance. One of his subjects stated, under hypnosis:

> *"Guides also comfort us during the trying periods in our lives, especially when we are children in need of solace. [...] Our personal guide helps us cope with the separateness and isolation which every soul inherits at physical birth, regardless of the degree of love extended by our family. These learned teachers remain with us over thousands of earth years to assist us in our trials before, during, and after countless lives... Their most important attribute is the ability to motivate you and instil courage."*

The role of spirit guides is not to solve all our problems. If they did, there would be scant possibility of us evolving and growing. Rather, they seem to illuminate pathways by providing us with clues and insights. But we need to be willing to change:

> *"Our teachers don't get perturbed with us to the point of alienation, but they have a way of making themselves scarce when disgruntled students avoid real problem-solving. Guides cannot assist in our progress until we are ready to make the necessary changes in order to take full advantage of life's opportunities."*

We are given room to make mistakes and make our own choices, for the purpose of 'growth' and the evolution of our soul:

> *"We gauge each situation. We know life is transitory. We are more... detached because without human bodies we are unencumbered by the immediacy of human emotion. As watchers in the stillness, we recognize the amount of... turbulence... from the wake of troubled thought. Then we carefully merge with it and gently touch the mind. You are shut out of a cluttered mind when attentions are distracted and thought energy is scattered all about. Watchers are not supposed to intrude. It's more of a... soft coupling. I implant ideas – which they assume is inspiration – to try and give them peace. I have to be careful not to spoil my people by making life too easy for them... to let them work out most of their difficulties without jumping right in..."*

Ultimately, separation is an illusion. We are all One... we are never *alone*.

* * * * * * * * *

Insight #2: You Are Magnificent And Powerful Beyond Your Imagination

Who you are is a part of *God*. You are an amazing, divine, eternal being. You never die. You go on forever. You are powerful beyond your imagination. You possess creative powers that allow you to manifest exactly what you want – what you *really* want, that is, subconsciously.

Your physical body is the body *you* chose for a very specific purpose in this lifetime. Be grateful for it. Take care of it. It is your 'vehicle for life'. It consists of trillions of cells that power your body every moment of your life; systems that work together seamlessly in unbelievably complex ways; thousands of miles of blood vessels; a brain that is more powerful than the most advanced supercomputer; a body that is a marvel of bioengineering. The most highly perfected robot ever created will never be more than a vulgar machine by comparison to the human body.

You are more beautiful than you know, more grand than you can imagine, more wealthy than you can dream of. You are all things. You are infinite possibility. You are creativity, love, compassion, kindness, joy, truth, and power. Every aspect of humankind is reflected and contained in *you*. You get to *choose* moment by moment who you want to be and what you want to express. You can choose something entirely different tomorrow, or even right now.

Dr John Demartini writes: *"You are made of pure vibrating light waves, which physicists call quanta. We've been given an extraordinary gift. Of all the places in the universe that we've explored, we've never come across anything more magnificent that the human body, brain, and spirit."* [...] *"There wasn't anything here before, so it must all have been created from the substance of the Creator Itself. So what are you? You are a tiny piece of the body of God. May you forever love so you may live up to it."* [...] *"We already are perfection, and we can't ever get away from it… all we're doing is waking up to the balanced perfection that already exists."*

Stewart Swerdlow echoes this statement, by saying: *"Take credit for who and what you are. You are part of the God-Mind and as such, are a part of a vast and magnificent level of consciousness."*

* * * * * * * * *

Insight #3: Gratitude and Love
Are The Keys To An Amazing Life

Since everything in our reality is 'energy' and *vibration*, the Law of Attraction states that *you attract what you think about most of the time*. If you feel grateful for who you are and what you *have*, you resonate at that frequency, and you will *attract* more things into your life to be grateful for. If you feel *love* for yourself and other people, you will attract more experiences where you feel *love and you feel loved*. I have found that, in my own life, when I share freely from my heart, unbelievable amounts of love and appreciation flood back my way. Conversely, whenever I do anything from a place of fear or anger, only situations that produce more fear and frustration manifest themselves in my life.

The quality of your life depends on your emotions, moment by moment. Are you a millionaire that feels angry all the time? Well, your quality of life sucks. Are you a minimum-wage worker that is grateful and appreciates every moment in their life? You have riches beyond compare.

Your life is the most extraordinary, most exquisite *gift* ever created. This reality exists for you to experience feelings, sensations, physical touch, tastes, incredible sights, joy, love, sadness, and a rainbow of emotions in between. Be grateful every day for this extraordinary gift of *life!*

Do not envy wealthy people or movie stars… God only knows what they went through in the past—or what life they will experience in the *future*—to balance out their good fortune in this lifetime. Besides, you can make that choice next time around, if you feel it would serve you. And finally, since separation is an illusion and we are all connected, they *are* you, anyway. So you might as well be happy for them!

> *"Obviously people are happier if they are able to appreciate what they have, whatever it is; and if they do not compare themselves with others; and if they can school their own moods. One of the most robust findings of happiness research: that people who believe in God are happier."*
>
> Professor Richard Layard, London School of Economics

* * * * * * * * * *

Insight #4: You Chose Your Parents, And Your Children Chose YOU

Your children *chose* to be born to you. The soul of your child *chose* this body, it chose you —its parents— it chose its body, and it chose these particular life circumstances, before even coming into this physical reality. The souls of your children chose you based on your mind-pattern and on the lessons they wanted to experience in this lifetime.

Most parents seem to ignore the fact that their babies come to them with their own little personalities. It is particularly obvious when a couple has twins; twins often display extremely different characters, personalities, and interests, despite being born to the same parents and having the same upbringing. Their *soul*-personality is shining through, with its own interests and mission. And it chose *you* to help facilitate that learning.

This also means that you shouldn't hold on to any resentment towards your parents. After all, *you chose them*! Michael Newton writes:

> *"The hard tasks we set for ourselves often begin in childhood. This is why considerable weight is given to family selection by the soul. The idea that each of us voluntarily agreed to be the children of a given set of parents before we came into this life is a difficult concept for some people to accept.*
>
> *Many of us have unresolved, hurtful memories of those near to us who should have offered protection and did not. We grow up thinking of ourselves as victims of family members whom we inherited without any choice in the matter. This assumption is wrong. When clients tell me how much they suffered from the actions of family members, my first question to their conscious mind is, "If you had not been exposed to this person as a child, what would you now lack in understanding?"*
>
> *There are spiritual reasons for our being raised as children around certain kinds of people, just as other people are designated to be near us as adults. Overcoming adversity in these relationships may mean we won't have to repeat certain abrasive alliances in future lives. Surviving such trials on Earth [...] enhances our identity as souls. [...] The souls of my subjects apparently select bodies which try to match their character flaws with human temperament for specific growth patterns."*

Walter Makichen was an intuitive healer with the ability to communicate with the souls of children who hadn't been born yet. He would see them as a bright green oval light hovering around their mother-to-be.

In a passage from his book *'Spirit Babies'*, he describes how his client—a woman named Dawn—had recently got married and was trying to decide if it was time to have a child. Walter saw a 'spirit baby' in her aura, but it was her husband, Jim, who had a karmic connection with the child. The spirit baby communicated that he had been Jim's brother and showed Walter an image of a young man diving into a lake and then disappearing. Jim's brother had drowned in a lake ten years ago and Jim had always felt responsible for his death. He would come back as their child to complete the karma of their relationship and help Jim heal.

In another passage from his book, Walter describes a client who was in his early fifties, Bob, who had just gotten married for the second time. He deeply wanted to have a child, so he asked Walter for some advice. Walter saw a candlelit room with the sounds of Tibetan monks chanting. When the chanting ended he followed an older monk attended by a young boy. Walter witnessed the older monk dying and saw the young boy begin to cry. Then, he was drawn back to the present time. In his client's aura he saw a 'spirit baby' wearing a saffron-coloured robe. The spirit went on to explain that he was that young boy Walter had seen with the older monk, *and Bob had been that monk in a previous life!* The spirit told Walter that he was there to be Bob's son, but that he didn't like Bob's first wife so he had been waiting for the "right" mother, so that he may be raised as a Buddhist.

Bob was shocked by these revelations. He told Walter that his first wife seriously disliked Buddhism and anything to do with meditation. On the other hand, his new wife was a devout Buddhist. Her spiritual beliefs created the proper karmic atmosphere for the conception of this child. That was also why it had taken Bob so long to realize that he wanted a child. Walter Makichen writes: *"It's no secret that children often stimulate their parents to re-examine their religious beliefs. I believe that in many cases this is a past life agreement between parent and child to remind parents of their spiritual heritage."*

In most of the cases where couples want to have children and are not getting pregnant, the soul of the baby is there… *but it is waiting for the right circumstances to be born into.* For example, the couple might be living in the city instead of the countryside, or the spirit baby doesn't feel wanted.

One couple we know couldn't get pregnant for 8 years. They moved to the countryside... and they got pregnant the next month! My client Jenny C. wrote to me: *"My friend and her husband tried for a baby for over 20 years. They were living in India at that time and their dreams started to fade over the years. They decided to emigrate to Australia. Without another thought of a baby and busy with their new environment, house, jobs, etc. lo and behold, Joy became pregnant, in her 40s(!) when they had totally given up hope and thought it was impossible!"*

In a case study from Walter Makichen's book, the spirit baby communicated: *"Mom needs to change... she is too focused on her career... [there is] no space in her life for babies..."*. In another reading, Walter could see the baby's soul was upset and didn't feel wanted. He could see the child sitting with its arms crossed. It communicated to him that the mother had had an abortion many years before. When he relayed this information to his client, she burst into tears, saying that it was true... She communicated to the spirit baby her deeply-held desire to become a mother. Within a few weeks she became pregnant!

> *"Remember, you chose your parents for a reason. There are no accidents. Some say that they did not ask to be born to a particular family, but this is not true. Before you enter into the womb, you personally choose the best possible environment that provides the lessons and experiences that you need. Never tell your parents that you did not ask to be born. Yes, you did!*
>
> *Any child that you bring into this world is attracted to your family by the mind-patterns of the parents. <u>If you have wonderful thoughts before, during, and after conception, you will attract a child of like mind</u>.*
>
> *The child will enter this physical world when he/she is ready. Any child that comes to you is by design and not by accident. Some people are afraid to have children because they do not want to recreate another version of themselves. They do not like themselves and fear another human being in the world who reflects that in their face all of the time. [...] You may not like their choices but you must encourage him/her to make his/her own choices."*
>
> Stewart Swerdlow, *Stewart Says*

* * * * * * * * * *

Insight #5: Everything Serves You

There is a perfect, intelligent, divine order to our lives. Keep in mind that you *chose* this life. If you are still beating yourself up for something you did in the past, realize how it served you and move on with your life. *Let Go of the Illusion That Anything In the Universe Is Not Exactly As It Should Be.* Everything that occurs in your life *serves* you in some way. Every crisis is a blessing. Every problem and challenge you encounter is really an opportunity for you to grow and transcend one of your life lessons.

Don't complain about your circumstances. Instead, ask yourself, *"How does this serve me? How does my lack of money serve me? How does my illness serve me? What good could come from this? What is the lesson here?"*

Begin to look for the other side of problems, and negative events in your life. Be thankful for your challenges. *That is how you master life!*

When I lost my job in 2003 and ended up being homeless in London for half a year, I thought it was the end of my world. Now, looking back, it was hitting rock bottom that propelled me to change my life, start my business, and make a difference. Losing one's job is really just the Universe telling you, *"OK now, you've been doing that long enough..."*.

> *"Every circumstance, person, place, thing, idea, and event that occurs in your life is miraculously guiding, directing, and leading you to that special grand something that is powerfully inspiring for you."*
>
> Dr. John Demartini

Once you gain the wisdom of seeing divine order in your life, the love that surrounds you and that wants the best for you, you will experience freedom and gratitude every day, in a way few people do. Relax, let go, and trust that you are taken care of. Trust that you are safe. Trust that you are loved no matter what. Every challenge is an opportunity to find out who you really are, to choose who you want to be in relation to that challenge, and to grow, expand, and become *more*. Every challenge that comes your way, remember to say: *"Thank you for my life."*

If you think your life is a mess, you simply don't have enough perspective on it yet. In time, this situation will make sense. Just keep going. If you don't like your current circumstances, then choose something else. Choose to create a different outcome. If you think your life is a mess, start by putting order to your *thinking*. Write down your goals. Write down your 'perfect life'. Write down your new affirmations. Meditate every day. Visualize your perfect outcome every day. Eliminate your negative and limiting beliefs. You are a creation-machine, so get *creating*.

> "It follows from the supreme perfection of God, that in creating the universe has chosen the best possible plan, in which there is the greatest variety together with the greatest order; the best arranged ground, place, time; the most results produced in the most simple ways; the most of power, knowledge, happiness and goodness the creatures that the universe could permit."
>
> Gottfried Wilhelm Leibniz

There Are No Victims

People who complain about their lot in life are usually looking for sympathy or an excuse to justify their life. By acting like a 'victim' they get to avoid taking responsibility for their life. They get to avoid making a 'mistake' or experiencing 'failure', because they have someone to blame for their life. If they surround themselves by other people of similar ilk, who keep reinforcing a mindset of 'victimization', they can remain stuck there for a very long time. By encouraging and rewarding their victim mindset you are disempowering them. You are reinforcing the idea that they *are* indeed a victim and that they are powerless to change their circumstances. The truth is that *they themselves* created this situation, and they—and only they—can change it.

It starts by taking responsibility for your life, changing your thinking—your beliefs, values, and thoughts—and raising your standards.

When someone tells me at my seminars, *"You know, I'm kind of in a similar situation like you were, broke, homeless…"* instead of giving them the 'Oh, poor you' spiel, I say: *"GREAT! That means you are way more likely to succeed, because you have nothing to lose!"* Or I might ask them, *"In what way did you create this situation? What beliefs do you have, that brought you to this place? What decisions did you make that got you into this? What are you learning from this?"*

Your Family Is PERFECT

All families are perfectly balanced to give all its members exactly what they need to grow and experience their life lessons. Thank your parents, regardless of what they did for you or *to* you. Live in gratitude, every day, in every moment, and marvel at the divine perfection of how your life unfolds perfectly, as you chose it to. Be grateful for all that occurs.

> *"Relax and Find Peace. The Ultimate Outcome Is Assured. [...] It will all come out all right in the end. You can't lose in this game. You can't go wrong. It's not part of the plan. There's no way not to get where you are going. There's no way to miss your destination. If God is your target, you're in luck, because God is so big, you can't miss."*
>
> Neale Donald Walsch, Conversations With God

Tragedy and Physical Ailments Help Us Progress *Faster*

As you go about your life, you might notice a severely disabled person, or someone in tragic living circumstances, and think, *'Oh, poor man…'*. But were you to have a more spiritual perspective on the matter, you may read that situation very differently indeed. Michael Newton writes:

> *"Blueprints for the next life vary in the degree of difficulty the soul-mind sets for itself. If we have just come off an easy life, making little interpersonal progress, <u>our soul might want to choose a person in the time cycle who will face heartache and perhaps tragedy</u>. It is not out of the ordinary for me to see someone who has skated through an unchallenging life overloading themselves with turmoil in the next one to catch up with their learning goals."* […]
> *"Many handicapped people think if it were not for a genetic mistake, or being the victim of an accidental injury which damaged their body, their lives would be more fulfilled. As heartless as this may sound, my cases show few real accidents involving body damage which don't fall under the free will of souls. As souls, we choose our bodies for a reason. <u>Living in a damaged body does not necessarily have to involve a karmic debt we are paying off because of past life responsibility for an injury to someone else</u>. […] It is difficult to tell a newly-injured person trying to cope with physical disablement that he or she has an opportunity to advance at a faster rate than those of us with healthy bodies and minds. This knowledge must come through self-discovery."*

In some cases, souls choose to reincarnate for a very brief time, to selflessly assist the souls of their parents:

> *"I had a case where my client had died from a birth defect early in his last life. I asked, "What was the purpose of your life ending when you were only a few days old?" He replied, "The lesson was for my parents, not me, and that's why I elected to come back for them as a filler." [...] In this case, the parents had abused and finally caused the death of a child when they were together in an earlier life. Although they were a loving couple in the last life of my client, these parents evidently needed to experience the grief of having a child they desperately wanted taken away from them. Experiencing the anguish from this terrible loss gave their souls a deeper insight into the effects of severing a blood bond."*

Souls may also choose to experience a tragedy in order develop a particular aspect of their character, such as humility, or to help another soul evolve or experience a specific character trait:

> *"I have found that souls essentially volunteer in advance for bodies who will have sudden fatal illnesses, are to be killed by someone, or come to an abrupt end of life with many others from a catastrophic event. Souls who become involved in these tragedies are not caught in the wrong place at the wrong time with a capricious God looking the other way. Every soul has a motive for the events in which it chooses to participate. One client told me his last life was planned in advance to end at seven years of age as an American Indian boy. He said, "I was looking for a short-burst lesson in humility and this life as a mistreated starving half-breed was enough."*

What Are Your Life Lessons?

Have you noticed any *patterns* in your life? Is there a consistent issue that keeps coming back again and again in your relationships? With friends? Co-workers? Your boss? Family members, perhaps? Ask yourself:

- ❏ *Why does this keep happening in my life?*
- ❏ *What is the life lesson that I need to learn here?*
- ❏ *What is my current behaviour, and what is the belief that I have, that is manifesting this issue over and over again?*
- ❏ *How can I learn from this? What reaction should I have instead?*

* * * * * * * * * *

Insight #6: Be Kind Towards Others

Quantum Physics now proves what the mystics have always said: We Are All One. Be kind to others, because in truth they *are* you. Harming others would only be doing harm to yourself. It is interesting to note that the Golden Rule in many religions is: *Do unto others as you would do unto yourself!*

People who have had near-death experiences, psychics, and past-life regression subjects confirm that there is no 'hell' and you don't get 'punished' in the afterlife. That is not to say there are no consequences. One of Michael Newton's clients revealed the following, under hypnosis:

> *"I knew one of those souls. He had hurt a girl... terribly... and did not re-join our group. There was extensive private study for him because he did so poorly while in that body. [...] Punishment is... a wrong interpretation... it is regeneration. The teachers are more strict with those who have been involved with cruelty. [...] My friend didn't go back with us... his friends... after this sad life where he hurt this girl. [He came through the same spiritual gateway as myself] but he did not meet with anybody... he went directly to a place where he was alone with the teacher. After awhile... not long... he returned to Earth again as a woman... where people were cruel... physically abusive... it was a deliberate choice... my friend needed to experience that. [...] He took what he had done... back onto himself... he blamed his own lack of skill to overcome the human failings. He asked to become an abused woman himself in the next life to gain understanding... to appreciate the damage he had done to the girl. [...] All souls go to one spirit world after death, where everyone is treated with patience and love. Souls whose influence was too weak to turn aside a human impulse to harm others will go into seclusion and must endure individual spiritual isolation for a while. This is not punishment, but rather [...] a time for cleansing and purifying – for the restructuring of self-awareness within these souls."*

Our soul tries to elevate the human mind above its aggressive and fear-based tendencies. It does not always succeed:

> *"Living on Earth is difficult, for the newer ones especially, because they go to Earth expecting to be treated fairly. When they aren't it's a shock. For some, it takes quite a few lives to get used to the earth body. The brain drives a lot of fear and violence into our souls. It's hard for us, but that's why we come to Earth... to overcome...".*

Michael Newton adds: "*Our spiritual masters constantly remind us that <u>because the human brain does not have an innate moral sense of ethics, conscience is the soul's responsibility</u>.*" We need to consciously make the choice of expressing more compassion. Instead of reacting with anger, ask yourself instead, "*What would love do now?*". Remember that living on Earth is not easy for anybody. Show the people you meet more compassion.

Those That Anger You Are Your Greatest Teachers

The people who push your buttons and make you feel angry the most are your greatest teachers. In truth, they represent parts of you that you have disowned. You are only ever angry, really, with *yourself*. They are merely reflecting something you don't like from within yourself.

Make a list of the people who make you feel angry, and write down the list of traits and characteristics that makes you angry about them. If you're honest, you might recognize areas where you still have some lessons to learn. You see in others only what exists inside of yourself.

Anger is simply a tool that your soul-personality uses to see itself. The physical world is a mirror of your inner thoughts and emotions. Let go of the emotions of anger and hate, as they consume a tremendous amount of energy, cause stress, and create illness in the body.

Forgive Your Parents

Aside from the obvious reasons, there are *spiritual* reasons for loving and be kind to your parents. For starters, *you chose them*. While in the spirit world, you could have chosen to be born in any era, in any place, to any parents, but you chose *your parents*. There must have been important reasons behind that choice. They must have been the best choice possible for you to achieve the outcomes that your soul chose for its evolution. And yes, this is true even in cases of abuse and violence.

Not loving and accepting your parents will impact your self-esteem and your life in a number of ways. Rejecting your parents is tantamount to rejecting a part of *yourself* — because they *are* a part of you. Perhaps it is time to simply accept that, like you, they are imperfect people, with their own issues, who did the best they could with the resources they had. Cut them some slack, and show them—and yourself—some compassion.

Whenever we make our parents out to be 'wrong', we're going to have challenges. Dr. John Demartini writes: *"I assure you that <u>anything you don't love about your past will affect your future</u>. Have you ever met anyone who condemned their first wife or husband and then went out and found another just like them? [...] To not love your own parents can take its toll on your life and well-being. It can even affect your heart if you try to fall back into your past angered illusion."*

As a man, if you make your father wrong, you're going to have problems in your career. If you make your mother wrong, you're going to have problems in your relationships. And vice-versa if you're a woman.

> *"And remember this: that which you condemn will condemn you, and that which you judge, you will one day become."*
>
> Neale Donald Walsch, *Conversations With God*

Forgive Your Spouse

The purpose of marriage is not 'happiness'. The purpose of marriage is to teach people how to fully love *themselves*, which includes accepting their owned *and disowned* selves (a disowned self is a sub-personality that is punished each time it arises into consciousness). <u>You tend to marry your disowned parts. And you tend to have children who will grow up to represent your disowned parts</u>. *Until you learn to love all aspects of you.*

Dr. John Demartini explains, in his book *'The Breakthrough Experience'*:

> *"You are a full-quantum being, but in your mind, you can be fooled and deny or disown half of yourself. <u>Ironically, whatever you disown in yourself you attract into your life in one form or another</u>. You marry your disowned parts, become business partners with them, and attract them as clients and friends. Whatever you don't want to see or appreciate in yourself, you keep attracting into your life until you learn to love it. You can't escape your full quantum."*

And Finally... Forgive Yourself

Remember this: you have always done the best you could, with the resources you have. *You are loved and cherished, dearly, forever. You have nothing to fear. You can't mess things up. There is nothing you can do wrong.*

* * * * * * * * * *

Insight #7: Only Love Is Real

Neurosurgeon Dr. Eben Alexander stated in his book *Proof of Heaven* that the message he received from his spirit guide, during the time he was in a coma, was that LOVE is the basis of *everything*:

> "Without using any words, she spoke to me. The message had three parts: "You are loved and cherished, dearly, forever. You have nothing to fear. There is nothing you can do wrong." If I had to boil it to one sentence: You are loved. And, to just one word: Love. <u>Love is, without a doubt, the basis of everything</u>. This is the reality of realities, the incomprehensibly glorious truth of truths that lives and breathes at the core of everything that exists or that ever will exist."

American psychiatrist Dr. Brian Weiss stated in his book *Only Love Is Real*, that during his out-of-body experience his spirit guide explained that we are 'beings of light and love', and that love inspires 'right action':

> "Remember that you are always loved. You are always protected, and you are never alone.... <u>You also are a being of light, of wisdom, of love</u>. And you can never be forgotten. You can never be overlooked or ignored. You are not your body; you are not your brain, not even your mind. <u>You are spirit. Spirit has no limits</u>, not the limit of the physical body nor of the reaches of the intellect or the mind."

> "As the vibrational energy of the spirit is slowed down so that more dense environments such as your three-dimensional plane can be experienced, the effect is for spirit to be crystallized and transformed into denser and denser bodies. The densest of all is the physical state. The vibrational rate is the slowest. Time appears faster in this state because it is inversely related to the vibrational rate. As the vibrational rate is increased, time slows down."

> "Teach them to experience. Remove their fear. Teach them to love and to help one another... <u>to reach out with love, to reach out with compassion, to help others... this is what you must do on your plane</u>."

> "Action becomes right action when it becomes action along the Way, along the Path toward God. All other paths are eventually blind alleys or illusions. [...] <u>Action that fosters justice and mercy and love and wisdom and the attributes we call godly or spiritual is inevitably right action</u>. The fruits of actions along the other paths are transient, illusory, and false. These fruits entrap and deceive, but they are not what we really desire."

So often we get side-tracked with seeking wealth and success, when in truth, what we really want is to express our divinity; to express our *love*. Brian Weiss's spirit guide also shared with him the following:

> "<u>Love is the ultimate answer</u>. Love is not an abstraction but an actual energy [...]. Just be loving. You are beginning to touch God within yourself. Feel loving. Express your love. [...] Love dissolves fear. You cannot be afraid when you are feeling love. Since everything is energy, and love encompasses all energies, all is love. This is a strong clue to the nature of God. [...] When you are loving and unafraid, you can forgive. You can forgive others, and you can forgive yourself. You begin to see with the proper perspective. Guilt and anger are reflections of the same fear. [...] They are unnecessary, damaging emotions. Forgive. This is an act of love. [...] It is the reaching out with love to help another that is important, not the results. Reach out with love. That is all you need to do. Love one another."

> "Ego is the transient, false self. You are not your body. You are not your brain. You are not your ego. You are greater than all of these. You need your ego to survive in the three-dimensional world, but you need only that part of the ego which processes information. The rest — pride, arrogance, fear — is worse than useless. The rest of the ego separates you from wisdom, joy, and God. You must transcend your ego and find your true self. <u>The true self is the permanent, deepest part of you. It is wise, loving, safe, and joyful</u>. You have reversed reality and illusion. Reality is the recognition of your immortality, divinity, and timelessness. Illusion is your transient three-dimensional world. This reversal is damaging to you. You yearn for the illusion of security instead of the security of wisdom and love. <u>You yearn to be accepted when, in reality, you can never be rejected</u>. Ego creates illusion and hides truth. Ego must be dissolved, then truth can be seen."

In Neale Donald Walsch's book *Conversations With God*, 'God' says:

> "You are, at the core of your wonderful Self, that aspect of divinity called love. (This is, by the way, the Truth of you.) [...] <u>Love is the ultimate reality. It is the only. The all. The feeling of love is your experience of God. In highest Truth, love is all there is, all there was, and all there ever will be</u>. When you move into the absolute, you move into love."

> "Let all those who have ears to hear, listen. For I tell you this: <u>at the critical juncture in all human relationships, there is only one question: WHAT WOULD LOVE DO NOW? No other question is relevant,</u>

<u>no other question is meaningful, no other question has any importance to your soul.</u> [...] *Most people continue to be engaged by another question altogether. Not, what is the highest choice, but, what is the most profitable? Or, how can I lose the least?"*

> *"When I speak of love, I am not speaking of some sentimental or weak response. I am speaking of that force which all of the great religions have seen as the supreme unifying principle of life. Love is somehow the key that unlocks the door which leads to ultimate reality."*
>
> Martin Luther King, Jr.

Dr. John Demartini came to the following conclusion, after reading more than 30,000 books and texts: we are here to love, grow, and express our divinity. *Love* is our true nature:

> "<u>There is nothing but love, and all else is illusion.</u> [...] *The universe is an infinite school of unending spiritual light. We're here to learn, teach, and become our true nature, love and light, and those closest to us are our greatest teachers in this school of life."* [...] *You're here on this planet to grow.* [...] *Inside every single person is an overwhelming desire to fully express their divinity, the absolutely spirit of love that they have and are.* [...] <u>Everything you do, good or bad, positive or negative, serves to teach you about love.</u>" [...] *We're here to love.* [...] *Did you know that your true nature, underneath all of your hopes, fears, thoughts, and feelings, is nothing but love and light? The universe has an inherent balance and order whose expression is this love and light.* [...] *Love is simply a state of nonseparation, where you perceive no division between yourself and some aspect of the world." (The Breakthrough Experience)*

David Icke had an out-of-body experience in 1993 after ingesting Ayahuasca in the Amazon rainforest. In that altered state of consciousness his spirit guide revealed to him that we are all part of 'Infinite Consciousness'. He writes in *Infinite Love Is The Only Truth*:

> *"Ayahuasca is known as the 'teacher plant' and the 'plant of the gods' ... The drug simply changes the nature of the decoding process and plugs you in to another information source... I went deeper and deeper through levels of consciousness until I reached a state of indescribable peace and bliss... All was stillness or sometimes like a slow-motion wave... The words emerged*

slowly and powerfully without any help from me. It began with 'I am love', and then, 'I am everything and everything is me, I am infinite possibility'. ... The words told of an Infinite Consciousness, referred to as 'The Infinite', 'Oneness' and the 'One'. Everything was Infinite Consciousness, the words said. Division and polarity were illusions... everything was One. There was no me or we, just an infinite 'I'. ... I was told that there was really only one thing I needed to know and these words began to repeat over and over in my head: <u>Infinite Love is the only truth — everything else is illusion</u>'."

Raymond Moody's near-death experience subjects and Michael Newton's past-life regression subjects revealed that upon our return to the spirit world we are asked about our journey towards being more loving...

"How did you learn to love and accept your fellow human beings in the way Source totally accepts and loves you?"

During my interview with 'The Miracle Man' (see Chapter 6), Glyn stated:

"Love is the source power that one needs to move forwards. Love is a catalyst to the greatness and the glory of the divine. [...] <u>Love is the greatest key to the human existence</u>."

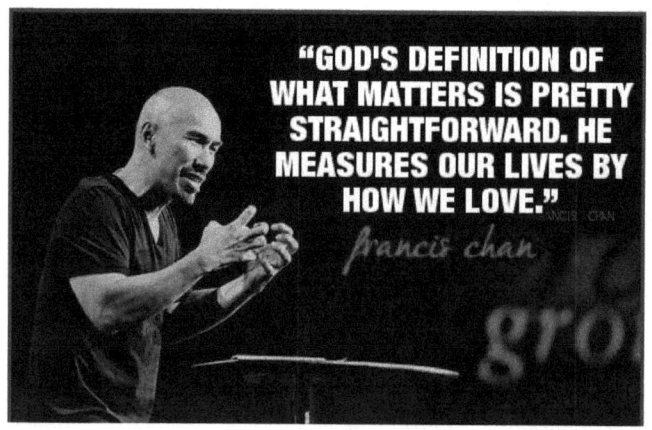

Love Brings Us Back To A State Of HEALTH

The spiritual channeller Barbara Marciniak states that love is what returns people to a state of health. She says: *"Understand that ill people are looking for love. There isn't enough love in their lives. It is LOVE that brings them back."*

Since everything is energy, and we are all vibrating at different frequencies, one can imagine that there is a particular frequency of health, and conversely there must exist a vibrational frequency of 'disease'. Marciniak hints at the intriguing possibility that a vibrational device could be invented, that restores health to people's bodies: *"Are there devices that can reproduce the LOVE FREQUENCY? When you can develop machines that can have frequencies adjusted so that they remind the body of its health and to restore the vibration of health, that CAN bring people back. Then they have to deal with the question 'Am I loved or am I not loved'?"*

Dr. John Demartini confirms the healing power of love. He writes: *"I've worked with terminal cancer patients who had spontaneous remissions, and in each case, some form of love and gratitude came into their lives and shifted them. A spiritual experience transformed their illness. Even watching a movie about love has been shown to increase the levels of immunoglobulin A in the saliva, the body's first line of immunological defence. We get ill to teach us to love. It's not a punishment or a mistake. It's a gift. [...] Illness is your body's way of telling you that you're lying about life. Every symptom and sign in your physical body is designed to reveal to you what you're lying about."*

Anger, fear, low self-worth, feelings of guilt, lack of self-expression, abandonment issues, and many other negative emotions (in other words, the opposite of 'love') manifest themselves as dis-ease in the body.

Come back to a state of *love*.

Let go of fear, and embrace love. Whenever faced with a challenge, a difficult decision to make, a fight or an argument... Ask yourself...

What Would Love Do Now?

* * * * * * * * * *

> "You have been taught to live in fear. You have been told about the survival of the fittest and the victory of the strongest and the success of the cleverest. Precious little is said about the glory of the most loving. [...] When you choose the action love sponsors, then will you do more that survive, then will you do more than win, then will you do more than succeed. Then will you experience the full glory of Who You Really Are, and who you can be."
>
> Neale Donald Walsch, *Conversations With God*

Insight #8: Find Your Purpose and Do What You Love!

When are you at your happiest and most fulfilled? When you are helping people and making a difference in their lives; when you are creating; and when you are connecting with people. *This is because who you really are is a creative, spiritual being having a human, physical experience, and we are all One*. Your essence is *love*. It stands to reason that you will feel happy, balanced, and fulfilled when you do things that are loving. This is why, if you are feeling 'stuck', the fastest way to get *unstuck* is to go do something nice for someone else! You find your equilibrium (and regain your health) when you start living in accordance to your true self and your highest values.

Michael Newton writes in *Journey of Souls* that advanced souls living among us display the following characteristics:

- Their fulfilment comes from improving the lives of others.
- They go about their works in a quiet, unassuming manner.
- They have an evenness of mood.
- Their interests are directed toward helping human progress.
- They display integrity in their life choices.
- They are rarely self-indulgent.
- They seek personal truths beyond the demands of ego.
- They seek to expand and achieve their potential.
- They are self-expressed.

Conversely, 'less advanced' souls do not take personal responsibility for their actions, they prefer to play the 'victim' game, and they do not demonstrate a generosity of spirit toward others.

In Buddhist tradition *giving* is seen as a path to happiness. *"Happiness comes when your work and words are of benefit to yourself and others"*; *"In seeking happiness for others, you find it for yourself"*, the Buddha teaches us. *"What is the meaning of life? To be happy and useful"*, says the Dalai Lama.

> *"If you want happiness for an hour, take a nap. If you want happiness for a day, go fishing. If you want happiness for a year, inherit a fortune. If you want happiness for a lifetime, help someone else."* (Chinese proverb)

Living An Authentic Life Brings You Happiness

We become fulfilled by living an *authentic* life. This means being true to ourselves by discovering our higher purpose and making a difference in people's lives.

Being on your purpose makes you feel fulfilled and happy. Having a purpose gives you focus, energy, and the power to break through your fears. Negative events, occurrences, setbacks, criticisms, etc. mean little to you because your *purpose* is unchanging, your determination unwavering. It doesn't matter what obstacles are encountered, you overcome them with ease when you are *on your purpose*.

> "Your soul doesn't care what you do for a living – and when your life is over, neither will you. Your soul cares only about what you are being while you are doing whatever you are doing." [...] "Go ahead and do what you really love to do! Do nothing else! You have so little time! How can you think of wasting a moment doing something for a living you don't like to do? What kind of living is that? That is not a living, that is a dying!"
>
> Neale Donald Walsch, *Conversations With God*

Abundance Comes To You When You *Give*

Interesting things happen in your life when you shift from a mindset of "entitlement" to one of gratitude and *giving*. I have found in my own life that *the more I give, the more good things come to me*. You may find that the things you have been trying to *get* for so long come to you when you start *to give*. Wealth, abundance, financial security, recognition, admiration, acceptance, love, self-esteem, confidence, peace of mind, gratitude… all showed up in my life when I stopped feeling entitled and stopped trying to *take* from my employer, for example, and instead began freely *giving*.

> "Why do you get up in the morning and go to work? 95% of people will answer 'I don't know! Everyone else does!' The Opposite Of Courage is Not Cowardice… It's Conformity."
>
> Earl Nightingale, *The Strangest Secret*

Do What You Love And The Money Will Follow

Being stuck in a job just for the sake of a paycheck is soul-destroying. Some of the best advice ever professed is simply this: *work at what you truly love to be doing, even if that work does not make you rich*. Not sure what career or profession to go for? Do what you love, and the money will follow. Do not be talked into doing a University degree for a profession you have no interest in, *just because it pays well* or because your parents want it. They may want you to be a doctor or take over the family business, but you love sports, or working with children. When you wake up every morning excited about your career, and looking forward to starting your day, then you will be happier, more positive, healthier, less stressed, and secure.

Everyone has something that they would *love* to do. Something they are talented at, and that comes naturally to them. *That* is your work. Your desires and dreams are trying to tell you something. Don't dismiss them. You are being communicated with. Honour the things you truly want deep down. These are clues as to your true life purpose. Start it part-time if necessary. You might face rejection, failure, and setbacks, but do not give up. Eventually your *"love work"* will become your full-time career. When something truly matches your frequency, it is always successful. Money is a secondary consideration, because if you do what you *love* then *that* in and of itself, brings you enjoyment and fulfilment.

When one loses their job, the Universe may be sending them a message: *That part of your life is done, there's nothing more for you to do or learn there; it's time for you to do something ELSE!* When people struggle to find work, it could be that what they are looking for simply doesn't match them anymore and their subconscious is pushing them in a different direction.

Ultimately, your soul does not care one iota what you do for a living and how much *money* you earn. They care about how much joy, happiness, and gratitude you experience and how much *love* you share with people.

Download your Special Report for FREE:
"How To Discover Your Life Purpose In 21 Minutes"
Go to www.ProsperityPower.com/purpose

Not Being On Your Purpose Can Lead To Illness

Bronnie Ware is a former nurse who worked in palliative care. In her book *The Top 5 Regrets of The Dying*, she revealed what people who were about to die regretted the most:

1. I wish I'd had the courage to live a life true to myself, not the life others expected of me;
2. I wish I didn't work so hard;
3. I wish I had stayed in touch with my friends;
4. I wish I'd had the courage to express my feelings;
5. I wish that I had let myself be happier.

Bronnie Ware adds that living with so much regret and bitterness led to them developing illnesses, too: *"Too many people suppressed their feelings in order to keep peace with others. As a result, they settled for a mediocre existence and never became who they were truly capable of becoming. <u>Many developed illnesses relating to the bitterness and resentment they carried as a result</u>."* In most instances these regrets stem from the single decision to focus on materialistic pursuits: *"I need to focus on my career and making money, and work hard to 'get ahead and keep up with the Johnsons', at the expense of love, family, friends, my purpose, and my own soul."*

The health consequences of not following your heart can be dire. Dr. John Demartini writes: *"[A stroke] psychosomatically represents a state of futility, a loss of will to push on, and no more details left within your life vision."* In another passage from his book, he adds: *"Psychosomatically, cancer is the body's last-ditch attempt to help you reclaim your life... to help you get in touch with your intuition and be who you are, not who you believe or perceive you should be. It is a last-ditch attempt to help you self-correct."*

If we lose our purpose and inspiration, we decay and die. As the proverb goes, where there is no vision, people perish. Cancer may very well be *one* way for your soul to tell you: *"Listen, if you're not going to follow your true life purpose, there's little reason for us to stick around here! We're outta here!"*

> "What will actually make us happy is when we start listening to our soul, listening to our heart! and when you don't... you experience CRISIS!"
>
> Jamie Passmore, intuitive

We saw in Chapter 2 the story of Anita Moorjani, who stated that her cancer was due to her not being true to herself. The moment she realized her own magnificence, and replaced all her fears with a deep feeling of love, she was healed. She writes: *"I'm at my most powerful when I allow myself to be who life intended me to be."*

She adds: *"It's one of the best-kept secrets of our time: the importance of self-love. I can't stress enough how important it is to cultivate a deep love affair with yourself. I don't recall ever being encouraged to cherish myself. … my* NDE *allowed me to realize that this was the key to my healing. …True joy and happiness could only be found by loving myself, going inward, following my heart, and doing what brought me joy."*

> "No one who went for their dream, regardless of whether they succeeded or not, regrets it. But you meet a lot of people, at the end of their lives, who say "Gosh, I wish I had had the courage to go after my dreams…"
>
> Anonymous

Listen To Your Heart And Live Authentically

You feel happy when you listen to your heart and you live in accordance to your true values. That's when you are being *authentic*. It also boosts your self-esteem no end. Self-esteem means having *esteem for oneself*. You build it by doing what's hard, pushing through obstacles, challenges, and your comfort zone to create the life that inspires you. No progress means no growth, and that is death to your spirit.

In your heart you *know* what you would love to do. The truth is that *you can do* it, because you are a powerful CREATOR, with infinitely more power than you give yourself credit for. Follow your heart and you will be happy. Don't follow it and you are setting yourself up for a life of frustration and regret.

It is better to have the whole world against you than your own soul.

* * * * * * * * * *

Insight #9: Go Within Or You Go Without

Michael Newton explains in his book that connecting to the divine on a daily basis can bring you reassurance, insight, and diving guidance:

> *"During our lives, especially in periods of great stress, most people feel the presence of someone watching out for them. [...] People who listen and encourage their inner voice <u>through quiet contemplation</u> say they feel a personal connection with an energy beyond themselves which offers support and reassurance."*

One of his subjects explains, under hypnosis, that while in the spirit world one of his roles was to help the incarnated souls on Earth when they called for 'spiritual help':

> *"[To get their spirit guide's attention and guidance on Earth], <u>first, they have to calm their minds and focus attention away from their immediate surroundings</u>. By silence... reaching inward... to fasten on their inner voice. That is how they call for spiritual help. <u>They must expand upon their inner consciousness to engage me on a central thought. [I reach back to someone in need of guidance] by whispering answers into their ear</u>!"*

I believe this is where the importance of meditation comes in. but that is not why *I* started meditating in 2015. I started meditating because of a Jerry Seinfeld video I watched online...

Jerry looked great, vibrant, healthy, not a day over 40. I even thought to myself, *"He looks great for a a guy in his 40's..."*. Imagine my surprise when I found out that he was 60 years old! Coincidentally, that same week, I had come across a clip about 'The Police' reunion tour, and couldn't help but notice how much younger—and healthier—Sting looked compared to his band mates. Sting was in his sixties, but didn't look a day older than 45. I did a quick search online to see if Jerry Seinfeld and Sting had something in common, and sure enough: they both meditate.

> *"We crucify ourselves between two thieves: regret for yesterday and fear of tomorrow."*
>
> — Fulton Oursler

Jerry Seinfeld has said the following about the benefits of meditation:

> *"More than money, more than love, more than just about anything, I love ENERGY. I love it and I pursue it, and I want more of it. Physical and mental energy to me is the greatest riches of human life. And meditating is like this free account of an endless amount of energy. It is like your body is a mobile phone, someone hands you a charger for the first time, and you go 'Oooh, so THAT'S how it's supposed to work!'"*

In 2014 I met a multimillionaire business turnaround expert from South Africa, while speaking at an event in Lithuania, and he mentioned to me in passing that during his lifetime he had felt at his best when he was meditating 20 minutes in the morning, and 20 minutes in the evening. It was another hint from the Universe that I ought to start meditating.

Close to 600 scientific studies have shown that transcendental meditation brings distinct improvements in health, including a decrease in stress and anxiety levels, improved sleep, vitality and energy levels increase, the ageing process slows down, blood pressure normalizes, chronic illnesses decrease, and creativity and the ability to focus increases.

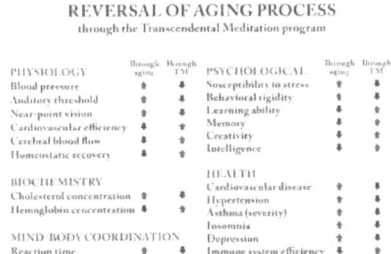
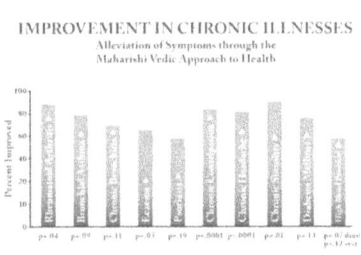

The people that I meet that are the most grounded, peaceful, content, and who emanate a beautiful 'energy' about them seem to all meditate. If there's something that is helping people improve their quality of life *that much*, it would be a shame not to apply it our life, don't you think?

Meditating has brought me another significant benefit: the experience of appreciating the present moment and being 'in the now'.

Most people in today's results-oriented and goal-oriented society tend to put off living. *"I'll be happy WHEN I finally achieve X…"*. Or worse still, they live *in the past*, burdened with neurotic feelings of guilt and regret.

> "One of the most tragic things I know about human nature is that all of us tend to put off living. We are all dreaming of some magical rose garden over the horizon...instead of enjoying the roses that are blooming outside our windows today."
>
> Dale Carnegie, self-improvement author and lecturer

Fear about the future —something that hasn't happened—or guilt and regret about the past —something you cannot change— are pointless, useless emotions. You cannot live in the past or in the future. You only get to live *in the now*.

The present moment is the only time you *really* have. You live, love, and experience *in the now*. Pay attention to your surroundings. Appreciate the beauty and nature all around you. The present moment is a *gift*. Be in the present moment. Pay attention to your life as it unfolds in the present.

Anita Moorjani writes: *"I felt strongly during my near-death experience that we're all connected to this Universal energy; we're all One with it. Each of us has this magnificent, magical life force coursing through every single cell. ...When we live completely from the mind over a period of time, we lose touch with the infinite self, and we feel lost. This happens when we're in <u>doing</u> mode all the time, rather than <u>being</u>."*

I meditate, at 10am and 4pm. I quieten my mind by focusing on my breathing. I empty my mind of all thoughts, and I enjoy being in the present moment. Whenever any thought comes into my mind, I 'swoosh' it away by using the words *"Come back to NOW..."*. This reminds me to come back to the present moment, and focus on my breathing again…

> "What I find surprising about Man, is that Man sacrifices his health in order to make money. Then he sacrifices money to recuperate his health. And then he is so anxious about the future that he does not enjoy the present; the result being that he does not live in the present or the future; he lives as if he is never going to die, and then dies having never really lived."
>
> The Dalai Lama

* * * * * * * * * *

Insight #10: Your Invisible World Creates Your Visible World

We now know that everything in the Universe is simply *energy*. Quantum Physicists proved that this energy is malleable to human intention. *Our thoughts and intentions can change our physical reality.*

For example, did you know that human intention affects the properties of water? Consistently, scientists have found that positive intentions focused on water containers that are later frozen tend to produce symmetric, well-formed, aesthetically pleasing ice crystals. Conversely, negative intentions tend to produce asymmetric, poorly formed and unattractive crystals.

Dr. Masaru Emoto in Japan performed experiments where he observed the crystals of frozen water after showing certain words or pictures to that water, playing music to it, or praying to it. The results were astounding.

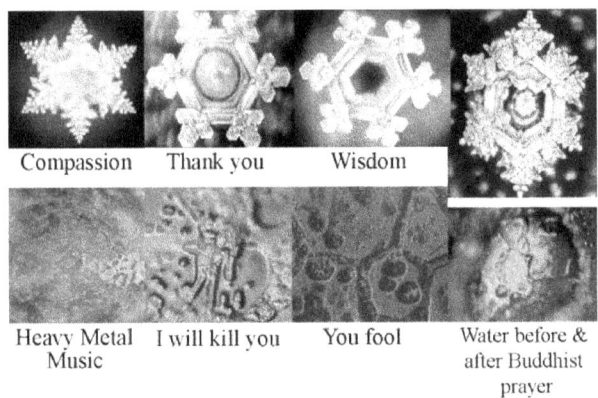

Water crystals after being shown positive and negative words

Mind Over Matter: You Can Use Your Mind To Heal

Since the human body is 70% water, one can imagine what negative emotions and thoughts do to our health. Which brings me to this point: You can use your mind to heal. Countless studies have shown how patients get healthy when given sugar pills and told this will cure them. Because they *believe* it will cure them, it does, when in fact the pills themselves have no effect on their bodies whatsoever. Our consciousness determines – to a large extent – what happens to our health (for example, hate and bitterness lead to the development of cancer, stomach ulcers, and many other physical illnesses, as seen earlier).

A Baylor School of Medicine study published in the *New England Journal of Medicine* conducted an experiment on patients with severe and debilitating knee pain. The patients were divided into three groups. In the first group, the surgeons actually shaved the damaged cartilage in the knee. For the second group they simply flushed out the knee joint, removing the material that was causing inflammation. These are the standard surgeries people go through who suffer from severe arthritic knees. The third group received a 'fake' surgery; the doctors merely made incisions on the knee and splashed salt water on the knee. The result? The placebo group improved just as much as the other two groups who had surgery!

In another example, in 1999 the United States Department of Health and Human Services reported that 50% of severely depressed patients taking drugs improved their mood, compared to 32% of those taking a placebo (and they didn't suffer any of the dreadful side-effects)!

Psychology professor Irving Kirsch from the University of Connecticut made some more shocking discoveries regarding antidepressants. He found that 80 percent of the effect of antidepressants, as measured in clinical trials, could be attributed to the placebo effect.

Curiously, researchers have found that the placebo effect is somehow getting stronger, with drugs such as Prozac now proving less effective than placebos – a worrying trend for pharmaceutical companies...

Plants Respond To Positive Human Attention

Many experiments show that the plants which get the most direct *positive* human attention, grow healthiest. Conversely, if you yell and scream abuse towards a plant, they wither and die, or fail to thrive. Our positive attention (and love) towards our plants is returned to us many-fold as they boost our strength when they are consumed.

Dr. Patrick MacManaway is the author of *"Energy Dowsing for Health"*. At a conference in Glastonbury, England, he revealed that his research showed that <u>animals gravitated to the water that had been blessed, and the crops and seeds watered by that water grew considerably more.</u> Through the use of 'subtle energies' and 'extended sensory awareness techniques' (meditation and focused intention, for example) he reports results such as a 20% increase in wheat and potato yields, 45% increase in sorghum yield, a 50% reduction in calf mortality, increased numbers of beneficial insects present, and many more astounding results.

Dr. Patrick MacManaway states: *"One of the greatest gifts we can give as humans is the gift of undivided, fully loving attention. When we give this to those around us, they and the space between us becomes filled with life and energy. We create an energy field within which things can thrive. The same applies when we extend our loving attention to the [plants and] animals in our life."*

Barbara Marciniak adds: *"The plant kingdom… it is essential that you focus on it. It will come into a much higher vibration, to help you. Not enough people say 'hello' to nature. You will eventually start talking to your plants, seeds, and flowers, to tell them what you need. Remember: nature supports you. so, communicate with it."*

<u>Our thoughts and intentions affect water particles, plants, animals, and people because *we are all part of one Consciousness and everything is mind energy!*</u>

Giving Thanks For Your Food Extends Your Longevity?

In the book *The Blue Zones*, author Dan Buettner identified longevity hotspots (the highest concentrations of centenarians) in Okinawa (Japan); Sardinia (Italy); Nicoya (Costa Rica); Icaria (Greece); and among the Seventh-day Adventists in Loma Linda, California.

One of the conclusions from his research was that people live longest in places where they are spiritually engaged, through prayer and giving thanks for their food; they have a strong sense of life purpose; and an engagement in family and social life.

Personally, I give thanks prior to a meal and I also say to myself this short prayer, recommended by Stewart Swerdlow:

> "We ask that what we drink or eat be blessed and cleansed by God-Mind for the most effective and efficient use by all levels of my body. I ask that my body keep only what it needs while allowing what it does not need to be eliminated. Thank you."

You Have The Power To Change Your Life

Look around you. Everything you see began as someone's idea or thought. The walls, the ceiling, the couch, the computer, the floorboards, the garden, the street, the car, the clothes you are wearing... all started as someone's thought! Everything around you began as *thought*. Why wouldn't it be the case for the Universe as well? (An atheist once argued to me that *"No! Some of the things I see around me are created by Nature!"* Right! But who do you think created Nature?!)

You have been creating your life so far, with your thoughts and your decisions. If you don't like how your life is going, <u>you can use your creative mind-power</u> *to change your life — by creating something new*. How? By writing down your goals. By becoming clear about what you really want. By visualizing exactly what you want. By using affirmations. By focusing on what you are grateful for. By reprogramming your subconscious mind with subliminal software. By flowing focused energy towards your desired outcome (what you focus on expands). It works!

You get your life to "take off" by being very clear about what you want to achieve. Have a clear and detailed plan for what you want to achieve in your life. The clearer you are, *the faster you will make it happen*.

> *"Visualize what you would love. The more detail you can envision, the more power you have. You are a co-creator, and the more vision and visualization you have, the greater your power to create. Imagine the finest details of what you would love to see. Can you see that any questions or obstacles that you might have are exactly the details you leave out? In much the same way, your uncertainty in life is directly proportionate to the details that you haven't questioned and answered. If you want to achieve self-mastery, you must ask the questions and get the details to master your life or you won't build it. The question is, are you important enough to yourself to take the time to plan?*
>
> *<u>"If you get absolutely crystal clear on exactly what you would love, and you can't see anything but that, it's almost impossible for you not to get it."</u>*
>
> John Demartini, *The Breakthrough Experience*

Your Invisible World Creates Your Visible World

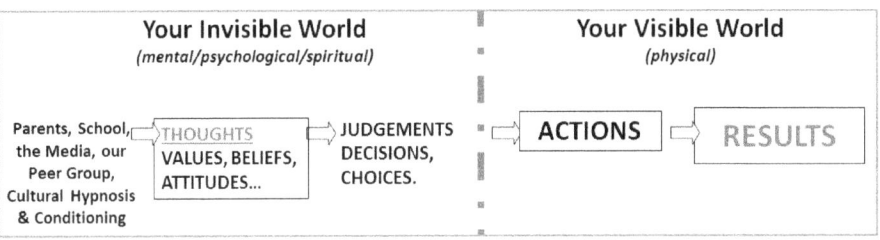

Most people believe that by simply changing their *actions*, their life will get better. The truth is that they need to go 'upstream', if they truly want to change their life: they need to first change their thoughts and beliefs. *Only then will their choices, decisions, and actions start producing different results. In fact, this will happen automatically.* For example, in my early twenties I identified and eliminated 44 limiting beliefs about money from my subconscious. Within a month I went from being broke to earning $10,000 a month. This also applies to relationships. For example, most women who are single have dozens of limiting beliefs about men and relationships. Your 'invisible world' (thoughts, beliefs) always creates your *visible* world.

> "I have established Laws in the universe that make it possible for you to have – to create – exactly what you choose. These Laws cannot be violated, nor can they be ignored. [...] The Laws are very simple: Thought is creative. Fear attracts like energy. Love is all there is. [...] The process of creation starts with thought – an idea, a visualization. Nothing exists in your world that did not first exist as pure thought. This is true of the Universe as well. Matter will form out of pure energy. In fact, it is the only way it can form. [...] I gave all My spirit children the same power to create which I have as the whole. Our essence is the same. We are the "same stuff"! With all the same properties and abilities – including the ability to create physical reality out of thin air."
>
> Neale Donald Walsch, *Conversations With God*

Have you ever noticed how negative people (who hold overwhelmingly negative thoughts) keep attracting more drama and problems in their lives? Their outer world reflects their *inner* world. They attract drama like a magnet. In order to transform their life they need to focus on gratitude, love, and cultivate positive thoughts and emotions in their daily life.

Aaron Scheinfeld, the billionaire founder of 'Manpower', once said: *"Andrew Carnegie, John D. Rockefeller, Henry Ford, Thomas Edison, and hundreds of the wealthiest industrialists of all time… had one thing in common. They all knew that… everything you see comes from the field of the INVISIBLE. And if you discover the secrets of how to use this invisible power, you can be, do, and have… anything."*

Brian Tracy wrote: *"Your outer world is a reflection of your inner world, and it corresponds to your dominant patterns of thinking. You become what you think about most of the time. Change your thinking, and you will change your life."*

> *"We live in a world of CAUSE and EFFECT. THOUGHTS are CAUSES, and your present conditions are the EFFECT. We must control our thoughts, in order to control our lives."*
>
> Earl Nightingale, *The Strangest Secret*

If you don't like how your life is going, you have to change your *thinking* first. Stewart Swerdlow explains: *"The bottom line is that you are responsible for totally everything in your life no matter what it is. This means you are never to blame anyone or anything else for your circumstances. What you think and feel is projected out and reflected back for you on every level. […] If you do not like the "movie" that is playing around you, then change the film, which is your mind-pattern".*

> "Thought is the first level of creation. Words are the second level of creation. Next comes action. […] You get your life to "take off" by first becoming very clear in your thinking about it. Think about what you want to be, do, and have. Think about it often until you are very clear about this. Then, think about nothing else. When your thoughts are clear and steadfast, begin to speak them as truths. Use the great command that calls forth creative power: I AM. "I am" is the strongest creative statement in the universe. Whatever you think, whatever you say, after the words "I am" calls them forth, brings them to you. There is no other way the Universe knows how to work. The Universe responds to "I am" as would a genie in a bottle."
>
> Neale Donald Walsch, *Conversations With God*

The Power of Our Intention

I understand the power that our thoughts have on our life. This is why I practice on a daily basis the art of 'conscious intention'. For example:

- The moment I wake up I set an intention for the day: *"I'm having an amazing day today!"*. You are more likely to have a great day, if you *intend* for it to be so.
- Before going to sleep, I write down my schedule for the next day. I *intend* for a productive day.
- I write down my goals. By doing so, they are more likely to manifest in physical reality. As Zig Ziglar states: *"The 3% of Yale graduates with specific written goals had accumulated more financial wealth than the other 97% of the class combined."*
- I have a detailed, written "Life Vision" describing my ideal life.
- Years ago I wrote down in detail my 'ideal partner'. As a result, I manifested an incredible woman into my life.
- I give thanks for my food, prior to every meal.
- I say my affirmations out loud every day, including expressing my gratitude for all the love, joy, and abundance in my life.
- I have the words 'Gratitude', 'Love', 'Peace', 'Joy' taped to our glass bottles and water filter.
- When I leave for a trip I visualize arriving at my destination on time, safe and sound.
- When I'm driving in a busy town I set an intention that the perfect parking space will await me at my destination. And it does.
- When I am travelling abroad or going on holiday, I write down exactly how I want our trip to go, including our safe return home.
- I write down my intentions prior to attending a meeting or event.
- Before Mira gave birth to our girls, we wrote a one-page intention describing how the birth would play out. The drive to the clinic, the room set-up, how the staff would be, how long the labour would last, how she wouldn't need any drugs or medical interventions... Everything happened as intended.

Remember: everything is energy, and this energy is malleable to your thoughts and intention!

* * * * * * * * * *

The Law of Attraction

"You become what you think about most of the time. Plant thoughts of good health, and abundance in the garden of your mind. Like energy attracts like energy... If you are in a positive mood, you tend to attract positive people, events, and circumstances... and it all begins with your thoughts. Your thoughts determine your physical world. If you have predominantly thoughts of lack, fear, or failure... that is what you are producing in your world. If you have constant thoughts of abundance, success, and love... that is what you will get most of. If you are stressed and hectic... your world will be stressed and hectic... But if you are peaceful and harmonious... life will keep bringing you things that will make you peaceful and harmonious. Life is a mirror reflecting back to us what we think. The mind is producing the physical world around us. Life is not happening 'to' you. Life is responding to you. Change your thoughts, and your world will change along with it."

Justin Perry, The Biggest Secret Of Man (The Law of Attraction)

Download your Special Report for FREE:

"How To Identify And Eliminate Your Limiting Beliefs, And Finally Get Your Life To Take Off!"

Go to www.ProsperityPower.com/beliefs

CHAPTER 8

How To Win The Game Of Life

Deep down we all know the 'secrets' to a life well lived. You win the game of life by doing what most people are unwilling to do... Do what is easy, and life becomes hard. Do what is hard, and life becomes easy.

The first and obvious step to winning the game of life is... you must learn to love yourself.

- ❑ Learn to love and accept yourself *completely*; You are worthy of love. You *are* love. This is the fundamental first step.
- ❑ Have total CLARITY about what you want. That is how your life gets to "take off". Write down your goals and Life Vision.
- ❑ Know exactly what you want, and focus only on what you want.
- ❑ Be grateful, no matter what happens; know that everything that happens serves you in some way. Write in a 'gratitude journal' or remind yourself of what you are grateful for at the end of each day. To those who are grateful, more is given.
- ❑ Meditate daily.
- ❑ Take care of your body and your health; exercise and stretch, daily.
- ❑ Demonstrate Integrity in everything you do.

- ☐ Live a life where you are true to yourself. Follow your heart. Do what you love!
- ☐ Live your life from a place of LOVE, rather than a place of Fear and Ego... Show love and compassion for others. Giving is the path to happiness.
- ☐ At the critical juncture in all human relationships, there is only one question: "What would LOVE do now?" *No other question is relevant, no other question is meaningful, no other question has any importance to your soul.*
- ☐ Take full responsibility for your thoughts, choices, actions, and your Life. You are the creator of your reality. If you don't like what you've manifested so far, create something else.
- ☐ Allow yourself to be happy. Once a week, or at least once a month, do something you really enjoy.
- ☐ Express your true feelings. Be fully self-expressed creatively.
- ☐ Let go of guilt and regret about the past. Let go of fear.
- ☐ Don't watch TV and don't read the news. It is negative, violent, and detracts your focus from what you want. It's mostly lies anyway!
- ☐ Don't work so hard.
- ☐ Stay in touch with your friends.
- ☐ Be in the now; appreciate every moment and savour the gift that is Life. :)

Now go out there and LIVE FEARLESSLY *and with* PASSION!

* * * * * * * * * *

FINAL THOUGHTS

Thousands of people have died and come back to life, and *told* us what is on the 'other side'. They confirmed there is life after death. They confirmed the existence of God and the spirit world. Hundreds of thousands of people have had profound, spiritual, 'out-of-body' experiences and have confirmed our spiritual origins. These are people from all walks of life, with absolutely nothing to gain personally from these revelations.

Their accounts echo the knowledge shared by mystics and deeply spiritual people for millennia. Past-life regression therapists have found the same information flow from the subconscious of their patients. Top secret military experiments on the subconscious of soldiers have also confirmed these fundamental truths. Quantum Physicists have also confirmed the metaphysical nature of our physical reality.

The smartest people I know are choosing to live *consciously*. They choose to use the creative powers of their mind in a very specific way to create a magnificent life, for themselves and for others. They choose to switch off their television set and spend more time with their friends and loved ones. They choose to meditate, connect with nature, visualize, and give thanks. They choose to contribute to their fellow man. And at all times they are grateful for this gift called *life*.

You Are Loved And Cherished Forever

I used to judge the world and people for not being 'spiritual' enough. If everyone would just be 'more spiritual' then all of the world's problems would end, I thought. But where would the fun be in that? I now realize that everything is exactly as it should be. The world's merely a stage, for us to have fun and be fully self-expressed. We are at exactly the level of awareness we are meant to be at, at this time.

Let's bring awareness and love to more people. Let's heal their hearts, their minds, and their bodies.

Take advantage of this incredible opportunity to be alive.

Truly live with passion.

Create a magnificent life.

And remember…

> You are loved and cherished, forever.
>
> > You have nothing to fear.
> >
> > > There is nothing you can do wrong.

Get in touch!

Feel free to send in your thoughts about this book, or your story of near-death experience or 'out-of-body' experience to:

info@prosperitypower.com

If you are interested in subscribing to our newsletter, attending one of our live seminars, getting some coaching, or joining us on one of our exclusive **Prosperity Power retreats**, visit www.ProsperityPower.com.

We look forward to hearing from you soon and meeting you in person at one of our live events in due course!

Appendix

The War On Consciousness

Why Reincarnation Was Removed From Religious Texts

When the Bible was commissioned in 325 AD at the Council of Nicaea by the ruling class of Rome, they didn't want their soldiers to believe that their murderous actions carried consequences in the afterlife. How would they be able to invade foreign lands and kill their fellow human beings at the behest of their rulers if they knew of the karmic implications of such actions? Reincarnation was deleted from the Bible for political reasons. Furthermore, when you omit reincarnation and its philosophical repercussions from a religion, *you can kill in the name of God*. Thus, you can expand the influence, power, and wealth of the Church. The Crusades, The Holy Inquisition, the colonial conquest of Africa, the genocide of 100 million Native Americans in both North and South America are ample examples as examples of that...

Furthermore, it is harder for the ruling class of a country to control its population through fear, if the people hold a belief that *they are powerful, divine beings, who never really die*. The threat of eternal damnation—should they not obey your diktats—is a very effective psychological tool of persuasion.

In addition, the ruling class have accumulated vast tracts of land, wealth, and corporations. Materialism is at the *core* of their personal values system. It is therefore in their interest to create a society in their image, which rewards and reflects materialistic values, allowing them to prosper further (since they are already outstanding at accumulating material wealth). If spiritual values were to flourish, with the idea that "We are all one", a natural consequence would be that the ruling class *divvy up their wealth* to the poorest people on the planet. Two billion people on our planet live on less than $2.5 a day. Currently, just 8 men hold as much as wealth as the bottom 3.5 billion *poorest*. World poverty can be eradicated with a budget of just $60bn a year. By comparison, the USA spends $500bn a year on its military, to protect and expand the wealth of its ruling class.

Materialistic values make the population less likely to revolt or be involved politically. Edward Bernays (Sigmund Freud's nephew and creator of the 'Public Relations' industry) explained that <u>by stimulating people's inner desires and then sating them with consumer products you</u>

can manage the irrational force of the masses. They would sublimate their inner, primitive, sexual and aggressive forces through the consumption of goods. He called it "The engineering of consent" (which in reality is the *"engineering of the avoidance of dissent"*). Its aims would be achieved through clever, subtle, and pervasive propaganda aimed at controlling the minds of the unknowing public.

Materialism divides a population in a 'dog-eat-dog' battle—the age-old 'divide and conquer' technique—where people compete with each other to gain status and money, and unleashes selfish and self-centered behaviour. It helps maintain the status quo, which is highly profitable to the ruling class.

Materialism ensures that people consume more and more, thus enriching the wealthiest corporations and oligarchs on the planet. It keeps the wheels of industry turning. Consumption would slow down dramatically if people were to realize that they are perfect and divine just the way they are, and that *everything they need is within them.* You don't need that bauble to impress the neighbours, when you realize we are all One.

Religions may have started with the right idea—to inspire people to follow spiritual precepts. But these movements were quickly subverted and taken over by the political rulers of that era. They would have never allowed for a spiritual movement to threaten their grip on power. Religions and atheism are designed for the same objective: to keep the masses ignorant and disconnected from truth, so that they may be easier to control and manipulate, for the benefit of the ruling class.

Once the influence of religion started to wane over the human population, the "War On Consciousness" was critical for maintaining the ruling class in power. As a result, through unrelenting cultural indoctrination at school and through the mass media, people become 'atheists' and adopt the 'Philosophy of Futility'.

Mainstream media (corporate-owned), mainstream Science (corporate-owned), and mainstream religions are all in the service of the ruling class. Their purpose is to control your mind through constant propaganda and disinformation.

TED Talks Censors Talks About Consciousness

"While TED is positioned as trendy and cool, it's actually just another vehicle of idea suppression ... attempting to keep humankind ignorant of the reality of consciousness, spirituality and the fact that our cosmos is far more than physical "stuff." If the history of science has taught us anything, it's that scientists are perpetually delusional in their belief that they know everything ... Anyone who challenges their view of reality, consciousness, materialism, cosmology, or origin of the species is immediately branded a heretic and attacked or censored. [...] Through its selective censorship of talks on consciousness, TED is making sure no one spreads the "dangerous" idea that you are a conscious being with a non-physical, spiritual component which is not bound by materialism. To really understand the desperation behind TED's censorship and attempted suppression of ideas from people like Hancock and Sheldrake, you first have to understand why the idea of consciousness is so incredibly dangerous to modern-day science. According to virtually all modern-day "conventional" scientists, all humans are biological robots who utterly lack consciousness. They insist there is no soul, no God and that all spirituality is complete bunk. Meditation and prayer are hoaxes, they insist, and there is no such thing as premonition, intuition or other psychic phenomena. The entire system of corporate-driven science that dominates the world today depends on this "materialistic" delusion of the world. If scientists admit a non-physical soul survives physical death, then the "scientific" pollution of the world with chemicals, mercury, GMOs and other toxins sounds downright sinful. [...] The very idea [of] consciousness threatens the power dominance of all conventional medical doctors. Fighting the idea of consciousness is essential to protecting the medical monopoly that enriches drugs-and-surgery doctors. [Scientists] sure don't want to be seen as ever being incorrect about anything. So they will defend their outmoded, flat-Earth delusions to their dying day ... holding back humanity from any real revolution in consciousness that's essential for helping humankind achieve lasting progress."

Mike Adams, www.naturalnews.com

Appendix

What Do Atheists Believe?

Atheism, in a broad sense, is the rejection of belief in the existence of God. Let's take a look at their 'compelling', 'scientific', 'rational', and 'logical' arguments.

Atheist Argument #1: ***"God does not exist because I have not seen Him."***

By 'Him' they mean the white man with a beard, on a cloud. What is ironic, is that we *are* God... but atheists ask for *physical proof!* What do atheists expect exactly, a Larry King interview? Will they only believe it if they see it on the 9 o'clock news? If you were *all physical matter across infinite Universes...* would *you* bother showing up on a cloud (or a TV studio, for that matter) to make a point?

Religious teachings are so deeply ingrained into people's minds (even in non-religious people)—the image of a bearded *man* in a robe, somewhere on a cloud—that they cannot fathom the enormity of what God-Mind really is (an all-encompassing consciousness).

Despite millions of people having had profound spiritual experiences confirming the existence of a spirit world orchestrated by divine intelligence, millions choose to ignore this overwhelming body of evidence, because they only believe what they are told on TV.

> "I'm not religious. I don't know if there's a God. That's all I can say, honestly, is: "I don't know." Some people think that they know that there isn't. That's a weird thing to think you can know. "Yeah, there's no God." Are you sure? "Yeah, no, there's no God." How do you know? "Because I didn't see Him."
>
> There's a vast universe! You can see for about 100 yards, when there's not a building in the way! How could you possibly... Did you look EVERYWHERE? Did you look in the downstairs bathroom? Where did you look so far? "No, I didn't see Him yet." I haven't seen 12 Years a Slave yet, it doesn't mean it doesn't exist! I'm just waiting until it comes out on cable."
>
> Louis CK, comedian, *Saturday Night Live*

Atheist Argument #2: *"There is a lack of empirical evidence."*

Empirical evidence is information acquired by observation through our physical senses or experimentation. In other words, because scientists can't 'measure' God or the spirit world, it doesn't exist. This is tantamount to saying *"We used a measuring tape to measure feelings and love. We have come to the conclusion that such feelings do not exist"*. That would be silly, right? The 'scientific method' is simply not the right tool for the job.

Admitting that Science has come no closer to understanding the nature of our reality in the past four hundred years seems to be a step beyond most scientists, who cling to their hopelessly outdated Newtonian worldview.

Atheist Argument #3: *"There is evil in the world, so obviously this proves there is no God. God does not exist because if He did there would be no pain or suffering."*

Why would the God-Mind create a world where everything is hunky-dory all the time? What would be the point of that? Where is the excitement in that? Where would free will come into play? Besides, without all the drama, we'd be bored, and our souls would have little opportunity to grow.

Atheist Argument #4: *"God does not exist because the Bible is wrong."*

According to researcher Tony Bushby in his book *The Bible Fraud*, the oldest remaining bible in the world is the "Sinai Bible", and over 14,100 changes have been made compared to the Bibles presented today. Religions were subverted and taken over by the ruling class for political purposes a long time ago. Many religious dogmas today have little to do with the truth of the spiritual world. Just because you don't believe in a specific book or text doesn't mean that God does not exist.

Atheist Argument #5: *"There is no God because a lot of people on our planet don't believe in God."*

If God is all-powerful, *He* would have everyone believe in *Him* and worship *Him*... What nonsense. God-Mind is neutral. It does not need you to believe in 'It' anymore than it needs fish to believe in water.

Appendix

Atheist Argument #6: **"There is no God because there are conflicting religions on our planet."**

Again, why would God *impose* a single religion on mankind? What about free will?

Atheist Argument #7: **"I was created by Nature, not by God, so God does not exist."**

Who do you think created *nature?* There are 100 billion stars per galaxy… There are 100 billion+ galaxies in our universe… and there is possibly an INFINITE number of Universes… Where do you think all the matter that makes up our Universe *comes from?* What do you think was there *before time began?* I find it astonishing that people don't consider these questions, don't think critically, and just take convenient 'Scientific Theories' as fact.

Atheist Argument #8: **"God is a convenient fairy-tale for uneducated, superstitious people. It's too good to be true. People want God to be true, so they imagined God. But God does not exist."**

On the contrary, it is much more convenient to believe in *nothing*, and therefore do whatever you want with no moral consideration. Most people fail to see how the corporate, materialistic worldview they have been indoctrinated with from a young age has formed their atheistic beliefs.

And that's it. That pretty much runs the gamut of atheists' arguments.

> "What atheists don't seem to grasp is that atheism is itself based on an act of faith: faith in the idea that there is nothing beyond our perceptions of existence. They have no more factual knowledge of what lay at the center of life than any of the religious acolytes they so fondly attack, yet their own hypocrisy is apparently lost on them. Ironically, there is far more scientific evidence of God and spiritual life than there is evidence against. So by the very standards many atheists hold dear, it is they who are peddling indoctrination rather than truth."
>
> Brandon Smith, founder of The Alternative Market Project

The Moral Vacuum and The Pursuit of Happiness

"If we look at the last hundred years, the most obvious change in our ideas has been <u>the decline in religious belief, caused by the progress of Darwinian science. This removed the sanction of the after-life</u>. However, for some time the effect of this change was masked by the rise of socialism as a moral code involving mutual obligation. But the failure of socialism-in-action <u>left a vacuum which has been filled by relatively untrammelled individualism</u>. As Robert Putnam has documented, this individualism has become the dominating ideology in Western culture since the late 1970s. [The idea that] that the pursuit of self-interest will lead via the invisible hand to the social optimum. Yet all our experience shows that this is wrong: <u>the pursuit of individual self-interest is not a good formula for personal happiness</u>. You will be happier if you also obtain happiness from the good fortunes of others. In fact, the doctrine that your main aim must be self-advancement is a formula for producing anxiety."

Professor Richard Layard – *What Would Make A Happier Society?*

Rupert Sheldrake – "The Science Delusion"

"The 'scientific worldview' is immensely influential because the sciences have been so successful. They touch all our lives through technologies and through modern medicine. Our intellectual world has been transformed by an immense expansion of knowledge, down into the most microscopic particles of matter and out into the vastness of space.

Yet in the second decade of the twenty-first century, when science and technology seem to be at the peak of their power, when their influence has spread all over the world and when their triumph seems indisputable, unexpected problems are disrupting the sciences from within. Most scientists take it for granted that these problems will eventually be solved by more research along established lines, but some, including myself, think they are symptoms of a deeper malaise.

In *The Science Delusion*, I argue that science is being held back by centuries-old assumptions that have hardened into dogmas.

The biggest scientific delusion of all is that science already knows the answers. Contemporary science is based on the claim that 'all reality is material or physical'. 'There is no reality but material reality'. 'Consciousness is a by-product of the physical activity of the brain'. 'Matter is unconscious'. 'Evolution is purposeless'. 'God exists only as an idea in human minds, and hence in human heads'.

These beliefs are powerful, not because most scientists think about them critically but because they don't. But the belief system that governs conventional scientific thinking is an act of faith, grounded in a nineteenth-century ideology. I believe that the sciences will be regenerated when they are liberated from the dogmas that constrict them.

Here are the ten core beliefs that most scientists take for granted.

1. Everything is essentially mechanical. Dogs, for example, are complex mechanisms, rather than living organisms with goals of their own. Even people are machines, 'lumbering robots', in Richard Dawkins's vivid phrase, with brains that are like genetically programmed computers.

2. All matter is unconscious. It has no inner life or subjectivity or point of view. Even human consciousness is an illusion produced by the material activities of brains.
3. The total amount of matter and energy is always the same (with the exception of the Big Bang, when all the matter and energy of the universe suddenly appeared).
4. The laws of nature are fixed. They are the same today as they were at the beginning, and they will stay the same for ever.
5. Nature is purposeless, and evolution has no goal or direction.
6. All biological inheritance is material, carried in the genetic material, DNA, and in other material structures.
7. Minds are inside heads and are nothing but the activities of brains. When you look at a tree, the image of the tree you are seeing is not 'out there', where it seems to be, but inside your brain.
8. Memories are stored as material traces in brains and are wiped out at death.
9. Unexplained phenomena like telepathy are illusory.
10. Mechanistic medicine is the only kind that really works.

Together, these beliefs make up the philosophy or ideology of materialism, whose central assumption is that everything is essentially material or physical, even minds. This belief-system became dominant within science in the late nineteenth century, and is now taken for granted. Many scientists are unaware that materialism is an assumption: they simply think of it as science, or the scientific view of reality, or the scientific worldview. They are not actually taught about it, or given a chance to discuss it. They absorb it by a kind of intellectual osmosis.

In everyday usage, materialism refers to a way of life devoted entirely to material interests, a preoccupation with wealth, possessions and luxury. These attitudes are no doubt encouraged by the materialist philosophy, which denies the existence of any spiritual realities or non-material goals, but in this book I am concerned with materialism's scientific claims, rather than its effects on lifestyles.

The credibility crunch for the 'scientific worldview': For more than two hundred years, materialists have promised that science will eventually explain everything in terms of physics and chemistry. Science will prove that living organisms are complex machines, minds are nothing but brain activity and nature is purposeless. Believers are sustained by the faith that scientific discoveries will justify their beliefs. The philosopher of science Karl Popper called this stance 'promissory materialism' because it depends on issuing promissory notes for discoveries not yet made. Despite all the achievements of science and technology, materialism is now facing a credibility crunch that was unimaginable in the twentieth century.

[…] Crick was also a militant atheist. They explained there were two major unsolved problems in biology: development and consciousness. They had not been solved because the people who worked on them were not molecular biologists – or very bright. Crick and Brenner were going to find the answers within ten years, or maybe twenty. Both tried their best. […] At his funeral, his son Michael said that what made him tick was not the desire to be famous, wealthy or popular, but 'to knock the final nail into the coffin of vitalism'. (Vitalism is the theory that living organisms are truly alive, and not explicable in terms of physics and chemistry alone.) Crick and Brenner failed. The problems of development and consciousness remain unsolved.

The fundamental proposition of materialism is that matter is the only reality. [However] leading journals such as Behavioural and Brain Sciences and the Journal of Consciousness Studies publish many articles that reveal deep problems with the materialist doctrine. In biology and psychology the credibility rating of materialism is falling.

[…] Materialism provided a seemingly simple, straightforward worldview in the late nineteenth century, but twenty-first-century science has left it behind. Its promises have not been fulfilled. I am convinced that the sciences are being held back by assumptions that have hardened into dogmas, maintained by powerful taboos. These beliefs protect the citadel of established science, but act as barriers against open-minded thinking."

Source: Introduction to Rupert Sheldrake's book *The Science Delusion*
www.sheldrake.org

Scientists Confirm That Darwin's Theory Of Evolution Is WRONG

Thousands of scientists, biologists, palaeontologists, from all over the world have come to the same conclusion: The Theory of Evolution is complete nonsense. And yet you hear little of this on television, and the school curriculum is not changed. It remains the 'mainstream' point of view. In fact, unwitting agents of disinformation such as Bill Nye (author of "Undeniable") and Richard Dawkins (author of "The Selfish Gene" and "The God Delusion") are celebrated and promoted by the media.

Darwin's Theory of Evolution, while indoctrinated into us in school from an early age, is simply utterly false. It has been disproved and debunked by thousands of scientists all over the world. But mainstream science has too much at stake to come out and admit it, publicly. The truth would shake both the scientific and religious and institutions to the ground...

The Theory of Evolution was never a scientific law or a law of biology. It was merely a "theory". In truth, while a species might become slightly different through selective breeding, it does not EVER become a whole different species. Dogs cannot be selectively bred until they become a donkey, for example.

The Theory of Evolution is a religious dogma in its own right, asking people to suspend their disbelief over and over again. We are asked to believe that *living* cells came from inorganic (non-living) matter, that lightning struck a pond of water causing several molecules to combine in a random way, which by chance resulted in a living cell. We are asked to believe that fish decided to throw themselves onto dry land and spontaneously grew legs. We are asked to believe that certain animals grew wings and became birds of flight. We are asked to believe that humans evolved from apes, when there are still apes in existence.

Appendix

The fossil record simply does not support the evolutionary theory. Fossils prove the sudden emergence of a new species out of nowhere, complete with characteristics unknown in any other species. The fossil record has no intermediate or transitional forms. For example, giant dinosaurs literally exploded onto the scene during the Triassic period. The fossil record shows no intermediate or transitional species. Where are the millions of years of fossils showing the transitional forms for dinosaurs? They do not exist, because the dinosaurs did not evolve.

The Theory of Evolution was developed in the 1800s before science had the evidence available to prove the theory false. Modern scientific discoveries are proving evolution to be impossible. No new scientific discoveries have been found to support the Theory of Evolution. In fact, the growth of biological knowledge is producing scientific facts that contradict the evolutionary theory.

The smallest living cell contains more than 60,000 proteins of 100 different configurations. The smallest single-cell creature has millions of atoms forming millions of molecules that must each be arranged in an exact pattern to provide the required functions. The cell has an energy-producing system, a protective housing, a reproductive system, and a central control system. This complexity required an intelligent design. It is much too complex to happen by chance. (Source: 9 Scientific Facts Prove the Theory of Evolution is False, www.humansarefree.com/2013/12/9-scienctific-facts-prove-theory-of.html)

We keep being presented with two absurd worldviews, for us to choose from: *"Creationism! God created the world in seven days!"* or… *"Darwinism! We've evolved from apes!"*

They are both lies. The first one obfuscates the truth about our true spiritual nature and how the God-Mind created our Universe. While the second one is so ridiculous that it is truly amazing that we gobbled it up hook, line, and sinker for so long.

The real agenda behind the selective promotion into humanity's consciousness of these two theories is to *hide* the third alternative. It polarizes the debate while hiding from the minds of the public **the idea of "Intelligent Design" and that advanced civilizations might have seeded life on our planet.**

The most startling discovery made by human genome researchers is the fact that 250 genes out of our 25,000 genes are unique and are not found in any other terrestrial life form. Geneticists have not been able to find any evolutionary basis or terrestrial source whatsoever for these genes. What does that mean? It confirms that our 250 unique genes must have come from "a higher species" and an extraterrestrial source! (source: Grace Powers' documentary *Monkey Blood*).

The Sumerian civilization in Mesopotamia (present-day Iran/Iraq) seems to have mushroomed out of nowhere. If you are to believe official "history", one day we are cavemen, the next day we have civilization, astronomy, writing, laws, and science. More than 10,000 Sumerian clay tablets have been found on these sites. What do they tell us about their history?

They describe how an advanced civilization came to Earth and genetically enhanced the DNA of an animal that they found in abundance on the continent of Africa—one that was genetically well adapted to the gravitational conditions of Earth—to create a slave race on our planet, to serve this extraterrestrial race. They kept altering the DNA of their creation until they were pleased with the results. This explains the different iterations of Man, from Neanderthal Man to Homo Sapiens Sapiens, and why no "missing links" have ever been found. We may be related to chimpanzees, but through genetic manipulation and intervention!

And where did the chimpanzees, or all other animal species for that matter, come from in the first place? According to authors Anton Parks, Erich von Däniken, Stewart Swerdlow, and other 'secret government' whistleblowers, life was seeded on this planet by advanced alien races. This is knowledge held by the highest echelons of our society. The first colonizers of our planet brought with them the DNA of mammalian, reptilian, aquatic (e.g. dolphin), insect life, as well as plant life, to our planet, for the purpose of terraforming.

The elite at the pinnacle of our society do not want the masses to know the truth about who they are, where they came from, and why they are here. It is much easier to maintain the status quo and their wealth and grip on power, if the masses remain ignorant. He who controls the past, controls the future. And he who controls the future, controls the present…

Liberation Theology

"Liberation theology" was an attempt to return to the gospel of the early church, when Christianity was a pacifist religion of the poor. It began as a movement within the Catholic Church in Latin America in the 1950s.

<u>Its proponents sought social justice, an end to poverty, and human rights</u>. They also fingered the Catholic Church hierarchy in South America as members of the same privileged class that had long been oppressing indigenous populations from the arrival of Pizarro (1524) onward.

The Vatican and the US government stepped in, attacked, and crushed the movement.

* * * * * * * * * *

An Alternative History of The Life Of Jesus Christ

In 1870 an Aramaic manuscript entitled "The Gospel of the Nazirenes" was found in a Tibetan monastery. It appears to have been written by Christ's disciples in the period immediately after his death. In many places <u>it contrasts sharply with the familiar story and message in the final version of the Bible. It includes startling passages that directly defend the tradition of reincarnation</u> (along with equally unfamiliar tales of Jesus' studying various mysteries in India, Persia and Egypt, tales of his marriage, and much more).

Always and everywhere throughout these writings, **the image of Jesus is one utterly dedicated to gentleness and loving care for others**. Many scenes involved Jesus rebuking someone for cruelly inflicting pain on others, whether people or animals.

According to Stewart Swerdlow, author of *"True Blood, Blue Blood"*, the true history of Jesus Christ is very different to what is related in the Bible. The following revelations may clash greatly with your current worldview. But know that this is the knowledge and truth that is held at the highest levels of our society, within governments, the military, and religious institutions. Our ruling class keep this knowledge secret. Humanity may soon be ready though to accept the existence of extra-terrestrial civilizations that have been in contact with Earth—and genetically engineered humanity.

Swerdlow reveals that approximately 2,000 years ago beings from the Sirius star constellation abducted a young woman from ancient Israel with extremely pure human genetics, and implanted her with a foetus genetically designed for a specific purpose. Today this woman is known as 'Mary', and this is why it is claimed that she was a virgin. She said that she had been 'visited by angels'.

Mary gave birth to a boy by the name of Emmanuel. As a young man, Emmanuel was removed from his mother, and taken to the Great Pyramid on the Giza Plateau. For the next two decades he would be instructed in ancient Atlantean/Egyptian mystery school knowledge, in preparation for his work. He was indoctrinated in ways to steer the masses away from negative influences. His orders were to inculcate the three strains of humanity that had the purest Lyraen genetics on Earth (human genetics from the Lyra star system). These were the Hebrews, the Germanic tribes, and the Northern Indian Aryans who now lived in the foothills of the Himalayas. All three peoples used a lion as their symbol.

Most of this information can be found in a 2,000-year-old, resin-encased document uncovered in Jerusalem by a Palestinian researcher. This researcher translated some of this document, now called *The Talmud of Emmanuel*, into Swiss German. He was murdered before he finished deciphering it, as these revelations would have destroyed the Catholic Church.

The entire crucifixion scenario was staged as a way to secrete the entire family out of Israel to a safe place. The Christ figure was drugged before being placed upon the cross. Then he was removed, revived, and shuttled off to India by way of Damascus. His mother went with him, and he lived for a very long time. His grave can be seen to this day in the city of Srinagar, in the province of Kashmir, a hotly contested territory between India and Pakistan. There are researchers who dispute this claim in order to nullify the importance of the true history of Emmanuel.

In the hills of the lower Himalayas, the small villages have legends and histories concerning Emmanuel, who sojourned there for many years. **These stories say that he lived until the age of 117, when he "gave up" his body.** The villagers do not believe he really died then either. Many people in remote Himalayan villages report that he bleeps in and out of physical reality at will, and is able to literally manifest such things as food and clothing out of the air.

This was reported to western civilization in the late 1800s and early 1900s by researcher Baird T. Spalding and his entourage who stayed in the area for a couple of decades, and wrote a series of books on the subject. In fact, this researcher lectured all over the United States before he died in the 1940s. His research encouraged Hitler to send teams of explorers to the area in the 1930s.

The doctrines of Emmanuel are very different from the Jesus of the known Testaments. He encouraged self-analysis, and said that material gains were fine as long as one received them honestly. Emmanuel married Mary Magdalene and had three children with her.

Emmanuel's criticism of the corruption he observed at the temples placed him, his children, and Mary Magdalene in physical danger. Mary did not get along with the Apostle Peter and did not want to stay in Israel. Emmanuel went to India with his oldest son to remove some of the danger from his family.

For the rest of the family going through Central Asia was too difficult for them, so they were sent by boat across the Mediterranean to an area that was hilly and fertile, yet difficult for the Romans to occupy due to local resistance. Mary Magdalene and her two youngest children, along with Joseph of Arimathea, Emmanuel's brother, set sail for the South of France. It is interesting to note that for many centuries part of the South of France was a Jewish kingdom. To this day certain villages in the South of France re-enact the arrival of Mary Magdalene onto their shores.

Appendix

www.ingramcontent.com/pod-product-compliance
Lightning Source LLC
Chambersburg PA
CBHW071409160426
42813CB00092B/3437/J